Microparticle Dynamics in Plasma

Freya Hall

Copyright © 2024 by Freya Hall

All rights reserved. No part of this book may be reproduced in any manner whatsoever without written permission except in the case of brief quotations embodied in critical articles and reviews.

First Printing, 2024

ABSTRACT

Complex plasma or dusty plasma is a plasma, consisting of small solid particles of typical size from a few nm to mm scale in diameter in plasma environment. Some of the known dusty plasma phenomena observed are planetary rings of planets (e.g., Saturn rings), comet tails, interstellar clouds, fusion reactors (Tokamak and Stellarator), and contamination in semiconductor industry. The presence of even a tiny number of dust particles in the microelectronics industry or in fusion reactors has become an urgent issue. Dust charge and Debye screening length are two important parameters of dusty/complex plasmas because they influence not only the Coulomb coupling parameter, but also the transport of dust grains in electric and magnetic fields, and interaction with nearby dust grains. Current dissertation involves four specific contributions in dusty plasma mainly focused on magnetized dusty plasma.

Firstly, one of the primary objectives of dissertation is plasma characterization of novel asymmetrical design of Dusty Plasma Experimental (DPEx-II) setup, which is used for observation and study of dust crystal formation. Three different probe diagnostics such as Langmuir Probe, Emissive Probe and double Langmuir Probe is used to find the plasma parameters under varying experimental parameters like DC voltage, vacuum pressure, temporal and spatial resolutions etc.

Secondly, sheath structure near emissive wall/probe is studied in presence of dust particles through numerically.

Thirdly, the charged dust particles collective effects result in the production of a dust crystal-like structure, which is of importance in physics, chemistry, and materials science. Experiments have shown that dust crystals grow in plasma with and without the application of an external magnetic field. However, there is a limitation of theoretical study on the production of dust crystals in plasma. Hence, a new mathematical model is proposed with magnetic field and validated with COMSOL simulation. The behavior of charge dust particles in the presence of a magnetic field (***B***) up to 6 T has been studied using numerical and computational methods. Simulating charged dust particles in the presence of ***B*** is done using the COMSOL Multiphysics software. Interaction of charged dust particles are measured from the scattering cross-section parameter derived from the mathematical modelling and plotted with varying ***B***. In both numerical and computational analyses of charged dust particles, it is proven that the scattering cross-section reduces as ***B*** increases. Furthermore, crystal like structure formation is observed at higher ***B*** and the results are backed up by previous experiments.

Lastly, experimental works of dusty plasma has also observed that dust particles produces new phenomena in plasma such as longitudinal and low frequency wave modes. This shows that charged dust particles not just interact with plasma (electrons and ions) but self consistently can alter the properties of plasma. Additionally, low frequency modes developed in plasma due to free energy from ion streaming past charged dust particle is a self-excited wave.

CONTENTS

LIST OF FIGURES
LIST OF TABLES
LIST OF SYMBOLS

1. **Introduction**   1-32
    1.1 Introduction to complex (dusty) plasma
        1.1.1   Fundamentals of Complex plasma
            1.1.1.1 Charging mechanism of dust particles
            1.1.1.2 Charging time and characteristic scale length
            1.1.1.3 Characteristic frequencies
            1.1.1.4 Charge dust potential and Quasi-neutrality condition
        1.1.2   Coupling parameter
        1.1.3   Forces of dust particle
    1.2 Review of Earlier Works
    1.3 Scope and Outline of thesis

2. **Experimental Setup, diagnostics, and plasma characterization**   33-63
    2.1 Introduction
    2.2 Experimental Setup
        2.2.1   Vacuum Chamber and Electrode Configurations
        2.2.2   Power supply and pumping systems
    2.3 Probe diagnostics
        2.3.1   Langmuir Probe
        2.3.2   Emissive Probe
            2.3.2.1 Methods of determining plasma potential from emissive probe
        2.3.3   Double Langmuir probe

2.4 Plasma Characterization
2.5 Conclusion

3. **Virtual cathode in presence of dust particles near emissive wall/electrode**   64-88
   3.1 Introduction
   3.2 Brief review of previous work
   3.3 Mathematical model
   3.4 Numerical Results and discussion
   3.5 Conclusion

4. **Scattering Cross-section of charged dust particles in magnetized plasma**   89-118
   4.1 Introduction
   4.2 Brief review of previous work
   4.3 Mathematical modelling
   4.4 Simulation setup
   4.5 Results & discussion
   4.6 Conclusion

5. **Dust acoustic instability (DAI): A quantitative analysis in presence of magnetic field**   119-129
   5.1 Introduction
   5.2 Analysis
   5.3 Summary & Reviews of work

6. **Summary and future scope of works**   130-136
   6.1 Future scope of the thesis

LIST OF FIGURES

1.1 The change in states of matter as energy is supplied to the system. For plasma state to achieve, gas must be heated to very high temperature such that atoms split into electrons and ions 2

1.2 Various applications of dusty plasma ranging from very large scale to even micro size scale. [Credit: Cometery Tails - Copyright 1997 Jerry Lodriguss; Asteroid zones - NASA/JPL-Caltech; Planetary rings - Image via Ron Miller; Semiconductor Industy – Merlino & Goree, Phys. Today; Fusion reactor - Andrey Shalpegin et.al., Nuclear Fusion; Ionsphere – ISS, NASA]. 4

1.3 Schematic view of Tokamak with poloidal & toroidal magnetic field coil used for confining high temperature plasma. This design is also the basis for producing fusion in ITER, France. (Image Courtesy: https://www.energy.gov/science/doe-explainstokamaks). 5

1.4 Schematic diagram of different charging mechanism of dust particles: (a) Collection of charge species from the plasma environment; (b) Secondary electron emission; (c) Thermionic emission; (d) Photoelectric emission; (e) field effect emission. 8

1.5 Schematic diagram of dust-in-plasma and dusty plasma. (a) dust in plasma with isolated dust particles in plasma ($a \gg \lambda_D$) (b) dusty plasma with dust cloud having numerous dust particles interacting with each other ($a < \lambda_D$). 12

1.6 Schematic diagram of the forces acting on the dust particles. Arrow shows the direction of forces acting on the dust particle. T_1 and T_2 are the different temperature of the particular plasma species where $T_1 > T_2$. 19

2.1 Schematic diagram of DPEx-II device with probe diagnostics. 35

2.2 (a) Schematic diagram of Langmuir Probe circuit. (b) Tungsten Probe with ceramic holder 37

2.3 An ideal I-V plot from the Langmuir probe in plasma. 38

2.4	(a) Hairpin structure of emissive probe (b) Real design structure of tungsten filament of 0.125 mm diameter and 10 mm length.	40
2.5	Theoretical I-V curve of an emissive probe. (Image Credit: Hershkowitz (1989) [17])	42
2.6	In the limit of zero emission method, I-V traces are drawn with increasing emission. (Image Credit: Sheehan et al. (2011) [27])	45
2.7	(a) Double Langmuir probe (b) Circuit diagram of double Langmuir probe	46
2.8	Pictorial presentation of I-V characteristics of double Langmuir probe	47
2.9	Schematic 3D design of DPEx-II device.	48
2.10	T_e measured at constant pressure 0.12 mbar with varying voltage. Probe is scanned through the length of cathode tray, taking starting point near anode to farther end of the cathode.	49
2.11	(a) n_e with various DC voltage at constant pressure of 0.12 mbar. Probe is measured along the length of vacuum chamber above the cathode tray.	50
2.11	(b) n_e with increase in gas pressure at constant V = 325 V	51
2.12	(a) V_f at constant pressure of 0.12 mbar measured along the length of the chamber.	52
2.12	(b) V_p at constant pressure of 0.12 mbar.	53
2.13	(a) V_f at increasing filament current with varying DC voltage for constant pressure of 0.12 mbar	54
2.13	(b) V_f for various gas pressure at constant 325 V	55
2.14	(a) Measurement of V_p and V_f at various radial position for 325 V and 375 V discharge voltages at constant pressure 0.12 mbar. Position 1 cm corresponds to the probe near the cathode and last position to away from cathode.	55
2.14	(b) V_p and V_f with increasing pressure at constant discharge voltage of 325 V.	56

2.15	(a) I-V curve of double Langmuir probe at constant pressure 0.12 mbar and at discharge voltages of 325 V and 375 V.	57
2.15	(b) I-V Curve of double Langmuir probe at constant discharge voltage of 325 V with varying pressure.	57
2.16	Measurement of T_e for various discharge voltage and pressure.	58
3.1	Schematic diagram of potential profile in plasma sheath with emissive wall in a typical plasma system.	65
3.2	Phase portrait space diagram of a normalized potential ϕ	72
3.3	Phase-space diagram between dimensionless electric field $\varepsilon(\phi)$ and normalized potential (ϕ) as in Eqn. (3.22). Solid line corresponds to generalized potential of Eqn. (3.23).	74
3.4	Phase space diagram for $f = 0$ and $\alpha = n_{rd}/n_0$. This diagram shows the physical solution of potential structure formation with increase in thermionic emission.	75
3.5	Potential difference as a function of wall temperature for different n_{d0} and α is plotted at $Z_d = 1$. Variance of potential difference at (a) $n_{d0} = 10^3$ cm^{-3} (b) $n_{d0} = 10^4$ cm^{-3} (c) $n_{d0} = 10^5$ cm^{-3} (d) $n_{d0} = 10^6$ cm^{-3}	77
3.6	Potential difference as a function of wall temperature for different dust density and α is plotted for $Z_d = 1000$. Variance of potential difference at (a) $n_{d0} = 10^1$ cm^{-3} (b) $n_{d0} = 10^2$ cm^{-3} (c) $n_{d0} = 10^3$ cm^{-3}	79
3.7	Plot of potential difference for $n_d = n_{d0}$ at various α. For $\alpha = 0.2$, $T_{w,th} = 2494$ °K; $\alpha = 0.4$, $T_{w,th} = 2573$ °K; $\alpha = 0.6$, $T_{w,th} = 2621$ °K; $\alpha = 0.8$, $T_{w,th} = 2656$ °K; $\alpha = 1.0$, $T_{w,th} = 2685$ °K are respective values for irrespective of n_d.	82
4.1	A typical laboratory scale setup at $\bm{B} = 0$ T and $\bm{E} = 20$ V in DC discharge conditions with different time. (a) Simulation setup (b) $t = 0.5$ s and (c) $t = 2$ s. Electrode is kept in the XY plane and vertical direction of the chamber is the Z-axis.	101
4.2	Simulation results for the movement of charged dust particles at $\bm{E_c} = 6$ V and $\bm{B} = 0$ T for $t = 0.5$ s	103

4.3	Spreading of charged dust particles between the electrodes at (a) $B = 0.25$ T and (b) $B = 1$ T, for the simulation time 0.5 s. Positional change of a particle with time is shown vertically.	104
4.4	Behavioral changes of charged dust grains between the electrode at (a) $B = 2$ T, $t = 0.5$ s, (b) $B = 4$ T, $t = 1$ min and (c) $B = 6$ T, $t = 1$ min. Positional change of a particle with time is shown vertically.	105
4.5	Scattering cross-section of dust particles at inner and outer point of the dust particle distribution from COMSOL	106
4.6	Floating potential of dust particles with increasing B for $T_e = 1$ eV and $T_i = 0.1$ eV.	107
4.7	Scattering cross-section of dust particles in terms of β w.r.t B	108

LIST OF TABLES

2.1 Measurements of plasma parameters by Langmuir probe with various DC voltages and pressure   52

LIST OF SYMBOLS

Symbol	Description	Unit
e	Charge of electron	C
k_B	Boltzmann constant	Fm^{-1}
λ_{Ds}	Debye length of s species	mm
T_s	Temperature of s species	eV
n_s	Density of species	m^{-3}
r_d	Dust particle radius	μm
m_s	Mass of the species	kg
a	Dust inter-particle distance	μm
ω_{ps}	Frequency of species	s^{-1}
Z_d	Dust charge number	-
ν_{sn}	Collision frequency of species with neutral atoms	s^{-1}
σ_s^n	Scattering cross-section of species with neutral atoms	m^2
φ_d	Dust surface potential	V
I_s	Current of species	A
C	Capacitance of spherical dust particle	V
Γ	Coulomb coupling parameter	-
E	Electric field	Vm^{-1}
B	Magnetic field	T
V_{Ts}	Thermal speed of species	ms^{-1}
V_f	Floating potential	V
V_p	Plasma potential	V
A_{probe}	Effective probe area	m^2
V_b	Bias potential	V
Q_d	Dust charge	C

ε_0	Permittivity of free space	Fm^{-1}
φ_s	Potential of species	V
C_{is}	Ion acoustic speed	mms^{-1}
Ω_{cs}	Gyro-frequency of species	$rads^{-1}$
r_{cs}	Larmor radius or gyro-radius of species	m
$\psi(r)$	Effective potential energy	-
χ	Scattering angle	rad
$Z(\zeta_s)$	Plasma dispersion function of species	-

CHAPTER 1

INTRODUCTION

From past century, subject physics has been explored in various different kinds of fields especially quantum mechanics, materials science, radiation physics and most importantly atomic physics has been exploited a lot. In this mean time, there was further addition of matter to the existed states of matter, such as plasma, Bose-Einstein condensate and so on. Irving Langmuir, an American chemist, coined the term "plasma" in 1928 to characterize the positive column region in the discharge tube containing about equal numbers of ions and electrons, resulting in a small space charge. Later on, it was discovered that in universe most of the matter coexisted in plasma as much as 95% of the matter (e.g., stars, planetary rings, Nebula, interstellar medium), and remaining 5% consisting of black matter, gas and dust particles. However, it is very hard to grasp the idea of plasma on planet earth since very few natural states of plasma exist for example lightning bolt, Neon gas in tube lights, Aurora Borealis on the northern part of Europe, middle region of fire flames, etc. Furthermore, subject "plasma" became potential to explore & understand the underlying physics of ionization and recombination of gaseous atoms or molecules.

Solid, Liquid and Gas are the states of matter. Each matter on subatomic level interacts with each other through molecules and atoms. Hence, when solid is heated the bond between atoms or molecules breaks and forms a liquid phase where loosely bound molecules or atoms are formed. Further, supply of heat to the liquid breaks the bond between molecules and becomes a free phase state of independent molecules or atoms. If we further heat gas phase at a very high temperature at an increasing rate, then atoms & molecules break down. Due to thermal agitation of atoms or molecules and with further collisions, gaseous phase becomes ionized by splitting into electrons and ions respectively. Hence, the state of gaseous phase consisting of charge particles electrons and ions with neutral atoms or molecules can be probably said as Plasma. A beautiful representation of this process is shown in Fig. 1.1. However, state of plasma should be in quasi-equilibrium to be termed as plasma otherwise recombination rate is higher in these conditions. Therefore, a plasma is a gas of charged species with neutral atoms in quasi-equilibrium state. However, not every gaseous medium with charged particles is termed as plasma. There are some basic conditions or set of laws, which define plasma from charged gaseous state.

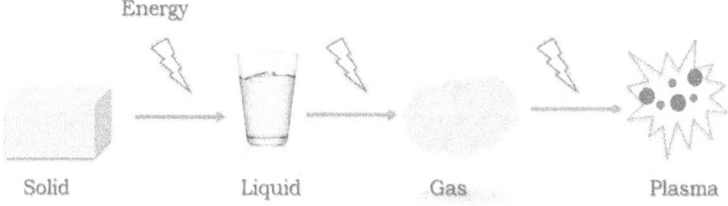

Fig. 1.1. The change in states of matter as energy is supplied to the system. For plasma state to achieve, gas must be heated to very high temperature such that splitting atoms into electrons and ions.

Dust particles are common in most of the plasma state, coexist alongside electrons, ions and neutral atoms. Dust particles acquire charges in plasma and becomes one of the components of plasma medium named as dusty plasma. Dusty plasma is also called as Complex plasma due to the various nonlinear phenomena associated which will be discussed later. Dusty plasma can be observed in many astrophysical phenomena such as galaxies, interstellar medium, Nebulae, cometary tails etc. In 1954, Hannes Alfven on "*On the origin of the Solar System*" critically considered that dust particles in solar nebulae might be the reason for formation of planets, stars and comets. Earlier during Second World War, in 1941 Lyman Spitzer put for the idea of the dust particles acquiring charges from the interstellar medium. Clearly, Langmuir, Spitzer & Alfven were the first to describe or understand the role of dust particles in plasma [1-3]. Similarly, dust particles were observed in semiconductor industry while producing chips. Moreover, dust particles are an impurity or unwanted in producing chips since it deteriorated the quality of chips [4-5]. Therefore, importance was given for developing clean rooms. Fig. 1.2 shows the various applications or process associated with the dusty plasma.

However, the attention towards dusty plasma was not achieved until the images from Voyager 2 was seen. Voyager 2 reveal the Saturn's ring system, which was reported by Morfill & Goertz [6-9]. For astronomers the field study of dusty plasma was a bridge to understand the phenomena observed in space whereas it was an inessential in semiconductor industry. Although, the observation of levitation of charged dust particles in RF power during process making of chips became a boon for plasma physicists. Therefore, dusty plasma offered a medium to investigate macroscopically through microscopic level, which offered a molecular study.

One of the important applications of plasma is the development of fully functioning of nuclear fusion plant for the generation of clean and environment friendly electricity for common uses. During Second World War, worldwide scientist did understand that the correct usage of fusion other than the producing or dropping hydrogen bombs. Two lighter atoms of tritium and deuterium are fused together at very high temperature of 1 million Kelvin producing a He gas. Process of fusion can be seen in stars and in many natural phenomena.

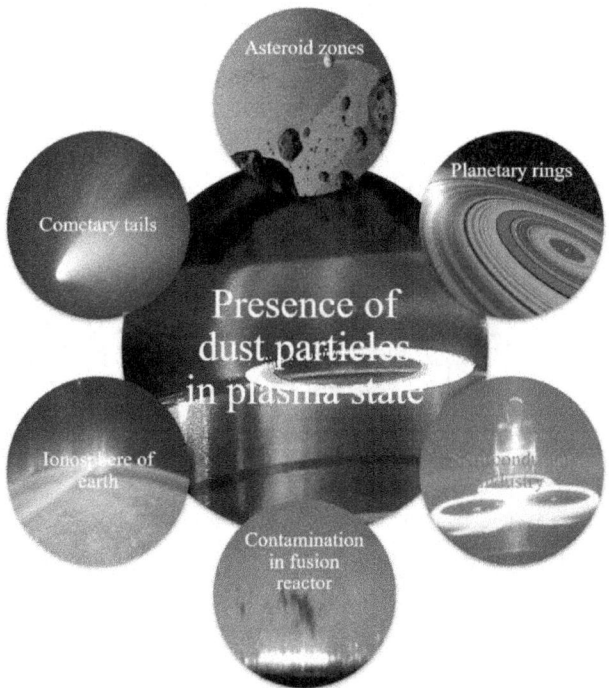

Fig. 1.2. Various applications of dusty plasma ranging from very large scale to even micro size scale. [Pic Credit: Cometery Tails - Copyright 1997 Jerry Lodriguss; Asteroid zones - NASA/JPL-Caltech; Planetary rings - Image via Ron Miller; Semiconductor Industy – Merlino & Goree, Phys. Today; Fusion reactor - Andrey Shalpegin *et.al.*, Nuclear Fusion; Ionsphere – ISS, NASA].

During fusion process, large amount of energy is produced, which are used for burning fuel etc. To make it possible, experimental fusion reactor was initiated and Russia is the first country to develop a fusion reactor prototype called '*Tokamak*' in late 1950s. It is donut like shape and plasma is confined with the help of magnetic field as shown in Fig. 1.3.

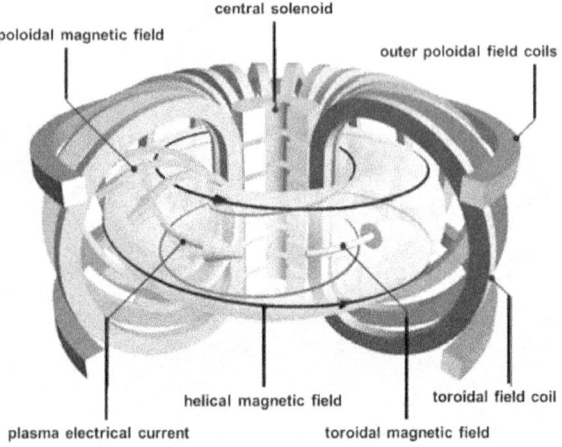

Fig. 1.3. Schematic view of Tokamak with poloidal & toroidal magnetic field coil used for confining high temperature plasma. This design is also the basis for producing fusion in ITER, France. (Image Credit: https://www.energy.gov/science/doe-explainstokamaks).

Generally, fusion in tokamak is established that at very high temperatures any solid material inside the reactor will be vaporized and ionized. However, confinement of plasma due to magnetic field especially at the edges i.e., near to the boundary surface played a key role in sustaining the plasma for a longer period. It was observed that at the edges, dust particles clearly sustained for a longer duration because the temperature at the edges are comparatively low than the center of the fusion process. Highly energetic particles escape the plasma and bombard the surface edges and form dust particles inside the device. Such bombardments are regular and large in quantity, so the scale of damaging the boundary surface and accumulation of dust particles poses a safety issues [10 - 13].

Applications of complex plasma has a varied range synonym to general plasma applications. One of the major applications of complex plasma apart from fusion process is ion thrusters. Ion thrusters are the propulsion system used for rockets, satellites, & spacecraft by using plasma as thrusters. Major problem of these thrusters is the accumulation of dust particles. When high beam of plasma ions is ejected out through the exhaust, the boundary material of exhaust is sputtered, and materials are eroded in small particles. These particles create an instability for an equilibrium plasma [14]. Hence, it is an especially important to understand the physics behind the complex plasma and associated phenomena.

1.1. INTRODUCTION TO COMPLEX (DUSTY) PLASMA

Apart from all the phenomena observed within the plasma, dusty plasma is an interesting topic of fundamental research. Size of the dust particle in plasma ranges from nanometers to millimeters typically. Contrary, dust particles in astrophysical phenomena are large ranging from meters to kilometer and heavy accumulation of charges on it. Dust particles are very large compared to the sizes of electrons, ions and atoms. Dust particles can be of conducting, metallic or insulating material and can vary in different shapes. In addition, these dust particles acquire charges from the surrounding plasma and become positive or negatively charged accordingly. Interestingly, comparing to the size of electron & ions to the dust particles, one can observe the behavioral pattern of molecular level structure of charged dust particles in plasma via illuminating through low power laser source. It is possible to track the individual positions and movement of the charged dust particles to maximum accuracy using the still images captured by the camera [15-16]. Hence, the formation of dust crystals or dust structures, and wave's instability lead plasma physicist to study the molecular behavior of dust particles in plasma.

1.1.1. FUNDAMENTALS OF COMPLEX PLASMA

Complex plasma can be looked in a different way if one tries to understand the underlying physics behind the phenomena (nonlinear) associated with it. Moreover, it is required to understand some fundamental concept related to dust particles in plasma. In the following sections, properties of dusty plasma like quasi-neutrality condition, dust-charging process, dust acoustic waves, coupling parameter, and characteristic scale lengths of dusty plasma are discussed in detail.

1.1.1.1 CHARGING MECHANISM OF DUST PARTICLES

As discussed in previous section, it is observed that how dust particles in plasma creates instability and hence quasi-neutrality condition. When dust particles are introduced in plasma, then they become charged from species (ions & electrons) of plasma. Dust particle can be negatively charged or positively charged according to the plasma environment or medium. In most of the laboratory plasma, dust particle gets negatively charged due to the lesser mass & higher mobility of electrons, compared to the massive & slow movement of ions. On the contrary to the astrophysical plasma, where presence of fast-moving ions makes dust particles positively charged [17-19]. Accumulation of charges on dust particle varies from 10^2 to 10^4 Q according to the electron temperature and plasma density. There is various mechanism for charging the dust particle in the plasma environment as shown in Fig. 1.4.

Collection of charged species.

Collection of charged species (electrons & ions) from the plasma is one of the primary sources of charging the dust particle. Charge on the dust particle can vary according to the size of the dust particle and plasma density. Electrons being lower mass and possessing much higher thermal speed than ions, foremost reach the surface of dust particle. Therefore, in early charging process, dust particle acquires large number of electrons from the plasma and hence becomes negative in potential with respect to bulk plasma.

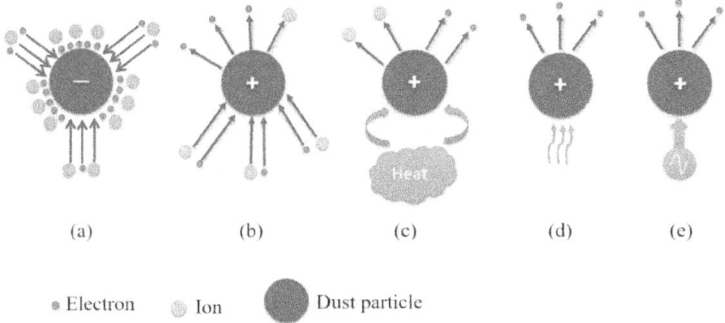

Fig. 1.4. Schematic diagram of different charging mechanism of dust particles: (a) Collection of charge species from the plasma environment; (b) Secondary electron emission; (c) Thermionic emission; (d) Photoelectric emission; (e) field effect emission.

In consequence, electrons are repelled, and ions get attracted towards the negative surface potential of dust particle. The magnitude of negative potential on dust particle becomes appropriately large that the flux of ions and electrons on to the surface of dust becomes same. As a result, the net current or flux of electrons and ions at the dust particle surface becomes zero. In other words, there is a sheath formation around the dust particle. However, dust charge is not constant, and it keeps fluctuating. Fluctuation of dust charge is one of the interesting phenomena to understand properly and currently research is going on.

Secondary electron emission

During the process of charging the dust particles, few fast-moving electrons bombard the surface of dust particles and release the electrons from the surface of dust particles. This process of bombarding energetic particle to the surface and removal of electrons is called as secondary electron emission as shown in Fig 1.4(b). Energetic particle can be both electrons and ions, depending on the plasma environment. The process of secondary electron emission is a distinct process that involves reflection, absorption, and transmission through electron impact on dust particle. Suppose an electron reach towards the dust particle surface, it faces a certain possible scenario i.e., getting reflected/scattered by dust grain, sticking to the dust particle surface and possibly enter into the dust particle interacting with one of the scattering centres and passing the energy to the dust material in the process of removal of electron from the dust surface material. Similarly, the process of ion impact on dust particle is same as electron impact. This process makes dust particles as positively charged.

Thermionic Emission

Phenomena of ejection of electrons & ions from the surface of material is known as thermionic emission. Similarly, ejection of electrons & ions is observed from the dust particle surface as shown in Fig. 1.4 (c). When dust particles are heated to high temperature induced through the hot filaments, thermal Infrared (IR) heating and laser heating etc. In this process, dust particle becomes positively charged.

Photoelectric emission

When a photon of energy ($h\upsilon$) falls on the surface of the dust particle and if the energy is greater than the work function of the dust material, then the electrons are emitted from the dust particle. This process is called photoelectron emission as shown in Fig. 1.4 (d). Emission will depend on wavelength of the incident light and surface properties of the dust particle. Ejection of electrons makes dust particle as positively charged [17].

Field effect emission

Sometimes dust particle in plasma becomes highly negative due to which electrons are emitted as field emission. There is a condition given by Whipple (1981) that if the surface electric field of dust particle is between 10^6 V cm^{-1} – 10^7 V cm^{-1} then field emission occurs. This process is shown in Fig. 1.4 (e).

1.1.1.2 CHARGING TIME AND CHARACTERISTICS SCALE LENGTH

Fluctuations of charge on dust particle is very common, so charge is not constant over the course of time. This can be attributed to the surrounding plasma conditions which itself is in a quasi-equilibrium state. When dust particle is introduced in plasma, the time required to get dust particle charged is called as charging time (τ_{ch}). In addition, it gives information about how rapidly the dust gets charged when plasma conditions are varied. Shukla & Mamun provide a brief calculation and equation, and it is observed τ_{ch} that varies inversely with dust radius and plasma density [17]. There are some other scales too, which are very significant and associated with dust particle in plasma. Initially the concept related to Debye length, dust radius and inter particle distance between dusts were discussed in detail.

Debye length

As of now, it is known that in a free space environment or phase space, plasma is a charged species of electrons & ions with neutral atoms in a quasi-equilibrium state. However, what happens if some external force or material is interacting with the plasma? Suppose, if any external force, potential, or material (dusts) is interacting (or in contact) with plasma, then charged species of plasma observes that the state of quasi-equilibrium is breaking down due to some external agency. As a result, charged species tries to shield the external potential or material forming as a sheath structure around that potential. It is the same phenomena as charging of dust particles. In dusty plasma, charged dust particles also takes part in shielding of any external field along with ions and electrons. Therefore, the strength of shielding of any external agency or matter is called as Debye shielding and it is measured by Debye length (λ_D). Debye length can be derived from the Poisson's equation and Debye length is derived as [17]

$$\lambda_D = \frac{\lambda_{De}\lambda_{Di}}{\sqrt{\lambda_{De}^2 + \lambda_{Di}^2}} \quad (1.1)$$

where $\lambda_{De,i}$ is the Debye length of electron & ion given as $\lambda_{De,i} = \sqrt{k_B T_{e,i}/4\pi n_{e,i0} e^2}$. $T_{e,i}$ is the electron and ion temperature and $n_{e0,i0}$ is the unperturbed electron and ion density. In a dusty plasma, with negatively charged dust particle $n_e \ll n_i$ & $T_e \gg T_i$ such that $\lambda_{De} \gg \lambda_{Di}$. This means that for this kind of dusty plasma λ_D can be determined from the density and temperature of ions. Contrary, for positively charged dust particle $n_e \gg n_i$ & $T_e \approx T_i$ such that $\lambda_{De} \ll \lambda_{Di}$ are the conditions for dusty plasma from λ_D can be determined from the density and temperature of electrons.

Dust particle radius and Inter dust particle spacing.

The change in associated properties of dusty plasma is dependent on dust particle radius (r_d). Looking at the case of the fundamental property of dust particle in plasma i.e., charging. Charging of the dust particle lot depends on the size of the dust, if it is large size then large number of charge species is accumulated on the surface and hence depletion of electrons in the bulk plasma creates ionization instability. Further, r_d is also key role in understanding the dust potential, studying cross-sectional collision with plasma species and forces acting on the dust particle. However, there are more than one dust particles inside the plasma and are separated by a distance called inter dust spacing (a). Generally, dust-to-dust interaction is through Coulomb interaction where surface charge of dusts interacts with each other. The screening of dust potential is limited to the dust Debye length (λ_D). Outside this screening length, the dust particles are isolated as shown in Fig. 1.5. Hence, a plasma with dust particles can be termed as '*dust in a plasma*' or '*dusty plasma*' depending on the distance between the dust particles, dust radius and dust Debye length. If $r_d \ll \lambda_D < a$, then plasma is a collection of an isolated dust particle with Debye sphere as shown in Fig. 1.5 (a). This system of isolated screened dust particle is called as 'dust in a plasma'. On the other hand, if $r_d \ll a < \lambda_D$, then the dust particles interact with each other crosslinking with each dust particle Debye sphere and acting as a collective behavior as shown in Fig. 1.5 (b). This system of forming dust clouds is called as dusty plasma. In both the cases, the charging process of dust particle changes but the philosophy of collection of charged species is same.

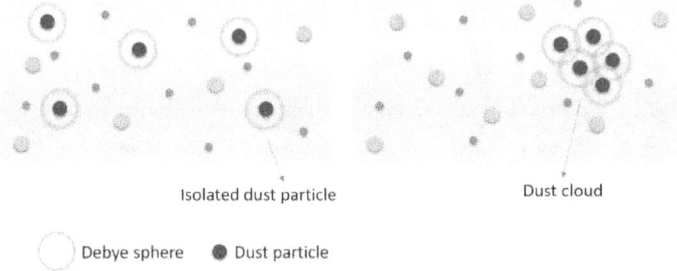

Fig. 1.5. Schematic diagram of dust-in-plasma and dusty plasma. (a) dust in plasma with isolated dust particles in plasma ($a \gg \lambda_D$) (b) dusty plasma with dust cloud having numerous dust particles interacting with each other ($a < \lambda_D$).

1.1.1.3 CHARACTERISTIC FREQUENCIES

In electron-ion plasma, electrons are considered as movable charge where ions act as a stationery background fluid. When some force field is applied to the plasma, the charged species tries to shield that force field to maintain its equilibrium state. Collective motions of electrons and ions tends to restore the neutrality condition. Therefore, there is displacement of electrons and ions from the equilibrium positions. This displacement of charged species give rise to the electrostatic oscillations in plasma, which is termed as plasma frequency [14]

$$\omega_{ps} = \sqrt{\frac{4\pi n_{s0} Q_s^2}{m_s}} \quad (1.2)$$

where s corresponds to the plasma charged species (electrons & ions). For an electron-ion plasma $Q_s = q$ since $Z = 1$.

In case of dusty plasma, when electrons and ions are displaced due to external force field, the charged dust particle being heavier pulls back the ions to equilibrium position. However, due to dust particles, ions get overshoot and oscillate around equilibrium position. Thus, charged species in plasma continuously oscillate around their equilibrium position. Similarly, for charged dust particles, dust oscillate around equilibrium position giving rise dust plasma frequency. The dust plasma frequency is given as $\omega_{pd} = \sqrt{4\pi n_{d0} Z_d^2 q^2/m_d}$. The oscillation frequency of ions, electrons and dust particles will not be same due to dependence of mass and charge of plasma species. Therefore, the difference between frequencies of each charged species becomes large i.e. $\omega_{pe} \gg \omega_{pi} \gg \omega_{pd}$.

Other than the electrons, ions and charged dust particles, there is neutral atoms present in the plasma. Collision of stationery neutral atoms with charged plasma species is also important. Ion-neutral collision frequency (v_{in}), electron-neutral collision frequency (v_{en}) and dust-neutral collision frequency (v_{dn}) are the respective frequencies. Therefore, collision frequency of neutral atoms with plasma charged species is given by

$$v_{sn} = n_n \sigma_s^n V_s \qquad (1.3)$$

where σ_s^n is a scattering cross-section mostly dependent on T_s, $V_s = \sqrt{v_s^2 + v_{ts}^2}$ is flow velocity of the plasma species, the thermal speed of the species $v_{ts} = \sqrt{k_B T_s/m_s}$ and n_n is neutral density. Due to the presence of neutral atoms and collisions, the oscillations of charged plasma species will be damped on a condition

$$v_{dn}, v_{in}, v_{en} < \omega_p \qquad (1.4)$$

1.1.1.4 CHARGED DUST POTENTIAL AND QUASI-NEUTRALITY CONDITION

In the earlier section of charging the dust particles in plasma through various process was discussed. In this section, how charge particles of plasma (electrons & ions) are collected by the dust particles will be discussed and the floating potential of dust particles. Similarly, for any probe diagnostics used for characterization of plasma is inserted into the plasma, the probe acquires first floating potential. Floating potential means equal amount of electron currents and ion currents to the probe surface ($I_e = I_i$). Dust particles behave similarly as a spherical electrical probe in a bulk plasma. Further, from floating potential one can determine the dust particle charge given as

$$\frac{dQ_d}{dt} = \sum_j I_j \qquad (1.5)$$

where j is for the plasma species (electrons & ions) and I_j is the current associated with that plasma species. Charging of currents (I_j) to the dust particle in plasma is given by the Orbital motion limited (OML) theory [20, 21]. Electrons and ions are assumed to obey the Maxwellian distribution. Collisionless plasma is assumed in OML theory due to mean free path of ions is much greater than the dust particle radius. The expression for charging currents to the negatively charged dust particles is given by [17-22]

$$I_e = -4\pi r_d^2 n_{e0} q \left(\frac{k_B T_e}{2\pi m_e}\right)^{1/2} \exp\left(\frac{q\varphi_d}{k_B T_e}\right) \qquad (1.6)$$

$$I_i = 4\pi r_d^2 n_{i0} q \left(\frac{k_B T_i}{2\pi m_i}\right)^{1/2} \left(1 - \frac{q\varphi_d}{k_B T_i}\right) \qquad (1.7)$$

where n_{e0}, n_{i0} are the equilibrium densities of electrons & ions, T_e, T_i are the electron & ion temperatures, φ_d is the surface potential, and m_e, m_i is the mass of electrons & ions. Exponential factor in Eqn. (1.6) is due to the repulsion of electrons from the negatively dust surface. OML theory is only applicable for a condition $r_d \ll \lambda_D$, where dust particle radius should be smaller than dust Debye length. Using Eqn. (1.5), (1.6) & (1.7), then dust charge equation is written as

$$\frac{dQ_d}{dt} = I_e + I_i \qquad (1.8)$$

At equilibrium, currents on the dust surface becomes zero i.e., $I_e + I_i = 0$, which is given as

$$1 - \frac{q\varphi_d}{k_B T_i} = \left(\frac{T_e m_i}{T_i m_e}\right)^{1/2} \exp\left(\frac{q\varphi_d}{k_B T_e}\right) \frac{n_{e0}}{n_{i0}} \qquad (1.9)$$

Therefore, the above equation can give the equation of dust surface potential. Now, because of electrons being higher mobility than ion in plasma, $\varphi_d < 0$. Dust charge is related to surface potential of dust by $Q_d = C\varphi_d$, where C is the capacitance of spherical dust particle given by $C = 4\pi\varepsilon_0 r_d \left(1 + \frac{r_d}{\lambda_D}\right)$. One thing to note about OML theory is that electrons and ions are collisionless and gives accurate results for the charge dust particle keeping in mind that mean free paths of electrons & ions are very larger than the plasma Debye length.

Charging time (τ_c) of dust particles in plasma can be determined from the Eqn. (1.8) where ion and electron current charge the dust particle. Charging time of dust is inversely proportional to the plasma density and size of the dust particles. Hence, fast charging occurs for larger dust particles and plasma having high densities. Accordingly, the charging time equation for negatively charged dust grain is given by

$$\tau_c = \frac{1}{\alpha_n [T_e/T_i + (V_{Te}/V_{Ti})\exp(-y_0)]}$$

where $\alpha_n \equiv Cr_d n_0/T_e$; C is the equation constant and y_0 is the equilibrium constant proportional to T_i/T_e.

Quasi-neutrality Condition

In an equilibrium plasma, the quasi-neutrality condition is given by $n_i \approx n_e$, which means plasma is macroscopically neutral. Similarly, when there is not any external perturbation to the dusty plasma becomes macroscopically neutral. Therefore, for dusty plasma charge neutrality condition is given by,

$$Q_i n_{i0} = q n_{e0} - Q_d n_{d0} \qquad (1.10)$$

where n_{d0} is the unperturbed dust density, $Q_i = Z_i q$ & $Q_d = -Z_d q$ is the dust particle charge; Z_d is the elementary charges collected by the dust particle. In most of the laboratory plasma, dust particles are negatively charged. Eqn. (1.10) can be more simplified as,

$$n_{i0} = n_{e0} + Z_d n_{d0} \qquad (1.11)$$

Due to absorption of electrons by dust particles, then the Eqn. (1.11) can be replaced by,

$$n_{i0} \approx Z_d n_{d0} \qquad (1.12)$$

However, complete absence of electrons is not possible because $n_{e0}/n_{i0} = \sqrt{m_e/m_i}$ when T_e & T_i are equal and $\varphi_d = 0$.

1.1.2 COUPLING PARAMETER

In a dusty plasma, highly charged dust particles give rise to distinct collective phenomena. One of the phenomena is strong electrostatic interaction between charged dust particles. The strength of interaction between charged dust particles is determined by the Coulomb coupling parameter (Γ). Coupling parameter also determines the formation of dust crystals in plasma. Coulomb coupling parameter can be defined as the ratio of dust potential energy to dust thermal energy and is given as,

$$\Gamma = \frac{Z_d^2 q^2}{a k_B T_d} exp\left(-\frac{a}{\lambda_D}\right) \qquad (1.13)$$

where dust thermal energy is $k_B T_d$. A dusty plasma can be categorized as weakly coupled system when $\Gamma \ll 1$ and strongly coupled system when $\Gamma \gg 1$. Hence, coupling parameter depends on number of charges on dust particle (Z_d), $k_B T_d$ and $-a/\lambda_D$ [23-26]. In most of the laboratory plasma, dust particles are strongly coupled plasma due to high Z_d and small a. Further, dusty plasma is also studied for phase transition of dust crystals by increasing or decreasing the dust temperature (T_d).

1.1.3 FORCES OF DUST PARTICLES

In laboratory dusty plasma, the motion of charged dust particles is the result of forces acting simultaneously. Electromagnetic force, ion drag force, gravitational force, thermophoretic force, neutral drag forces etc., are some of the examples, which act on the dust particles in plasma. A schematic diagram of forces acting on the dust particles is shown in Fig. 1.6.

Gravitational force

This force generally comes into the affect due to the large mass of dust particle. Gravitational force on charged dust particle of mass (m_d) acting downwards is given as [17, 27]

$$\vec{F_g} = m_d g = \frac{4}{3}\pi r_d^3 \rho_d g \qquad (1.14)$$

where ρ_d is the mass density of dust particle and g is the acceleration of gravity.

Electromagnetic force

A sum of the electrostatic force

$$\vec{F_E} = Q_d \vec{E} \qquad (1.15)$$

and Lorentz force is given by,

$$\vec{F_L} = Q_d(\vec{v_d} \times \vec{B}) \qquad (1.16)$$

gives the electromagnetic force on charged dust particles [17]

$$\vec{F_{EL}} = \vec{F_E} + \vec{F_L} = Q_d(\vec{E} + \vec{v_d} \times \vec{B}) \qquad (1.17)$$

where **E** and **B** are the electric and magnetic field and v_d is the dust velocity.

Ion drag force

Drag force can be termed as rate of momentum transfer of plasma species (electrons, ions & neutral atoms) to the dust particles or rate of momentum transfer of charge dust particles to plasma species. Hence, there two types of drag forces in dusty plasma, namely ion drag force and neutral drag force. Ion drag force are the sum of the rate of momentum transfer of positive ions to the dust particles through collection of ions, electrostatic Coulomb collision and positive ion flow effects [17].

$$F_{id} = F_{id}^{Coll} + F_{id}^{coul} + F_{id}^{flow} \quad (1.18)$$

where F_{id}^{coll} is the force due to collection of positive ions, F_{id}^{Coul} is the force due to electrostatic Coulomb collision and F_{id}^{flow} is the force due to the positive ions flow through dust particle respectively. F_{id}^{flow} can be neglected due to the complexity of equations to solve and it is very small contribution compared to the other two forces. Coulomb collision force and collection force is calculated as follows [17]

$$F_{id}^{Coll,Coul} = n_i m_i \sigma^{Coll,Coul} V_{it} v_i \quad (1.19)$$

where total ion speed is given by $V_{it} = (v_i^2 + 8k_B T_i/\pi m_i)^{1/2}$ and σ^{coll} is the collection cross-section in terms of dust surface potential and ion kinetic energy $(m_i v_i^2/2)$ given as [17],

$$\sigma^{coll} = \pi r_d^2 \left(1 - \frac{2q\varphi_d}{m_i v_i^2}\right) \quad (1.20)$$

Therefore, the collection force is written as,

$$F_{id}^{coll} = \pi r_d^2 n_i m_i V_{it} v_i \left(1 - \frac{2q\varphi_d}{m_i v_i^2}\right) \quad (1.21)$$

From Coulomb theory, one can calculate the momentum transfer cross-section as [28, 29]

$$\sigma^{Coul} = 4\pi b_0^2 \int_{b_c}^{\lambda_{De}} \frac{b\,db}{b_0^2 + b^2} \qquad (1.22)$$

where b is the impact parameter and b_0 is the impact radius corresponding to the 90° deflection given as,

$$b_0 = r_d \frac{q\varphi_d}{m_i v_i^2} \qquad (1.23)$$

and b_c is the direct collision impact parameter.

$$b_c = r_d \left(1 - \frac{2q\varphi_d}{m_i v_i^2}\right)^{\frac{1}{2}} \qquad (1.24)$$

After integrating the Eqn. (1.22), Coulomb force is rewritten as,

$$F_{id}^{Coul} = 2\pi b_0^2 n_i m_i V_{it} v_i \ln\left(\frac{b_0^2 + \lambda_{De}^2}{b_0^2 + b_c^2}\right) \qquad (1.25)$$

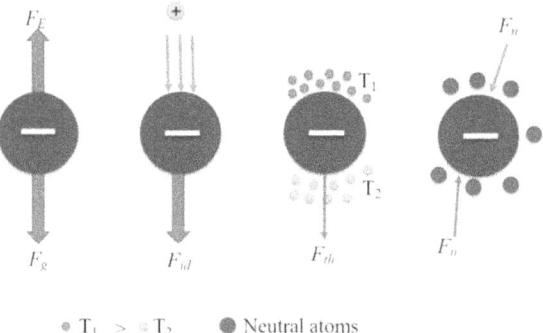

Fig. 1.6. Schematic diagram of the forces acting on the dust particles. Arrow shows the direction of forces acting on the dust particle. T_1 and T_2 are the different temperature of the particular plasma species where $T_1 > T_2$.

Neutral drag force

Neutral drag force is generated when there is collision interaction or momentum exchange between dust particles and neutrals takes place. The relative velocity between the dust particle and neutrals $v_r = v_d - v_n$ provides the basis for neutral drag force. It can be simplified that for $r_d \ll \lambda_{mfp}$, (where λ_{mfp} is the collision mean free path) and $v_d \ll v_{Tn}$ (where v_{Tn} is thermal velocity of neutrals), there is a neutral drag force experienced by the dust particle and can be given by Epstein's equation [17, 30]

$$F_{dn} = -m_d v_{dn} v_d \qquad (1.26)$$

where v_{dn} is the dust-neutral friction frequency and is given as [17]

$$v_{dn} = \frac{8}{3}\sqrt{2\pi} r_d^2 \frac{m_n}{m_d} n_n v_{Tn} \left(1 + \frac{\pi}{8}\right) \qquad (1.27)$$

where m_n, n_n & v_{Tn} are the mass, density, and velocity of neutral atoms.

Thermophoretic force

If there are two different temperatures of gas present in the plasma, then the dust particle experiences a temperature gradient force exerting from the higher temperature to lower temperature gas region. Such force is called as thermophoretic force generally towards the lower temperature gas region [31, 32].

$$F_{th} = -\frac{32}{15} \frac{r_d^2}{v_{th,n}} \left(1 + \frac{5\pi}{32}(1-\alpha)\right) \kappa_T \nabla T_n \qquad (1.28)$$

where T_n is the neutral temperature and κ_T is the translational thermal conductivity of gas. Accommodation coefficient (α) is close to unity for dust particles.

1.2 REVIEW OF EARLIER WORKS

Dust particles in plasma acquires charges and interact with the plasma species as well as with other dust particles. This leads to the various phenomena originated in plasma medium. In 1986, Ikezi predicted that the large number of charges acquired by the dust particles forms a crystalline structure [33]. This can be verified from the coupling parameter discussed in earlier section, which generally has a large value for dust particles to form crystalline structure. In most of the experimental work, dusty plasma is produced in radio frequency (RF) and direct current (DC) discharge plasmas. Dust particles are introduced and are levitated in the sheath region in one of the electrodes [34]. For a 10 µm dust particle, elementary charges acquired is of the order of 10^4 Q [35, 36]. Barkan *et al.* and Thomas *et al.* produced dust crystallization in RF discharge plasma [25, 37]. Since then, dust crystallization in plasma has been studied vividly [35]. One of the important factors to be understood is the charge to mass ratio of dust particle or in general of plasma species. Electrons in the plasma are the first to be magnetized under the effect of few mT and ions at slightly higher 100mT. Whereas for charge dust particles, remarkably high magnetic field is required to make it magnetized despite having high elementary charges because they have low charge to mass ratio [38, 39]. However, this gives an advantage to study the dynamic behavior of dust particles in magnetized plasma with high resolution camera. Due to magnetized dusty plasma, the charging currents to the dust particles alters. It gives an edge to study the individual dust particle dynamics under the influence of external force fields. Screening length of dust particle changes and its interaction to nearby charged dust particles. While the behavior of dust particles in magnetized plasma helps to understand the dust particles in fusion reactors, where at the edge of the fusion reactor lots of dust particles are accumulated due to the retention of tritium. These dust particles become problem in sustenance of plasma in the fusion reactor. Magnetic field of the fusion reactor plays a major part in containing the plasma. So, it becomes necessary to study the dynamical behavior of charged dust particles in magnetized plasma.

Laboratory plasmas or dusty plasma is majorly controlled by gas discharge parameters i.e., voltage applied between the electrodes and pressure of chamber. Dynamics of dust particles can be studied through high-speed camera by capturing the images of levitated charged dust. In early dusty plasma experiments, many researchers commonly used RF setup [25, 38-42] for plasma production. Only a few numbers of experiments were performed in DC setup [43, 44]. This different kind of setup using in the dusty plasma setup is due to the heating of dust particles by ion streaming and dust charging phenomena. In RF setup, ions don't respond to the high frequency electric field, while in DC setup dynamics of ions are affected by the cathode sheath region [45-48]. The first observation of dust Coulomb crystal in DC glow discharge plasma setup was achieved by DPEx device [49].

Collective phenomena of charged dust particles in plasma is one of the interesting and broadly open subject to explore in various laboratory dusty plasma system. Formation of virtual cathode near to the wall/electrode has been well known concept since the 1929 [50, 51]. Langmuir observed that due to space charge accumulation near the electrode, the accurate measurement of plasma potential was not possible. He observed that there is deep negative potential well, formed near the electrode. This gave the term virtual cathode in dusty plasma configuration. However, for a longer time major focused was to develop a theory to understand the formation of virtual cathode [52-54]. Plasma potential is the basic plasma characteristics to understand how plasma spatially varied in the chamber. One of the popular methods to measure the plasma potential is the probe diagnostics i.e., intruding external material in plasma to study the local parameters with varying applied potential [55, 56]. However, the theory and diagnostic technique are still a challenging in terms of measuring the plasma potential in very high-density plasma.

After the Ikezi prediction, there was a lot of buzz around the plasma physicists to really understand the role of dust particles in plasma physics. It is well known that collective phenomena of plasma species give rise to the different kinds of wave modes in plasma both longitudinal and transverse waves such as ion acoustic wave (IAW), electrostatic ion cyclotron (EIC), Ion acoustic shock waves (IASW) etc., [14]. Charged dust particles being heavy and slow response to the change in force field, produces low frequency wave modes in dusty plasma such as dust acoustic waves (DAW), dust ion acoustic waves (DIAW), dust lattice wave (DLW) etc., [57, 58]. Studies of these low frequency wave modes helps in understanding the wave-particle interaction and dusty plasma parameters especially in astrophysical environments such as planet's rings. After theoretical prediction of DAW by Rao *et al.* [59] and experimentally observed by Barkan *et al.* [60], DAW has been vividly studied by various groups and researchers [61-63]. DAW and IAW are very similar in comparison where in DAW inertia is provided by the dust particles and restoring force by the plasma species. The linear theories very well describe the small amplitude wave modes. However, for an unstable mode having larger amplitude, nonlinearities come into effect. These nonlinearities generate nonlinear structures like shocks, solitons (both oscillatory and monotonic), vortices etc., [61]. DIA solitary wave was first predicted by Bharuthram & Shukla [64] and later experimentally confirmed by Nakamura & Sarma [65]. Similarly, Dust acoustic shock waves (DASW), Dust acoustic (DA) solitary waves, Dust ion acoustic shock waves etc. were studied extensively theoretically and experimentally [58]. These linear and nonlinear waves are studied in dusty plasma without magnetic field. At high magnetic fields, when dust particles are magnetized, new or existing dust wave modes are modified. A lot of theories have put forth to understand modes dust wave in dusty plasma but very few have been explored both in theory and experiment specifically in the presence of magnetic field.

1.3 SCOPE AND OUTLINE OF THESIS

This thesis addresses the gaps in theoretical works of dusty plasma with the help of numerical and simulation methods. Initially, especially designed dusty plasma device called dusty plasma experimental setup (DPEx-II) similar to the DPEx has been characterized by three different probe diagnostic techniques to understand the plasma potential variance in spatial and temporal. DPEx-II is mainly used to study the Coulomb structure of dust through various densities, potential and its associated properties. The collective phenomena of charge dust particles in dusty plasma have been studied in presence of magnetic fields. Further, dust wave modes are studied in presence of magnetic fields with nonlinear parameters. Broadly, the objective of thesis can be categorized as

- To design and fabricate three different probes for a novel DPEx-II device and determining plasma parameters for various discharge conditions.

- To numerically analyse and visualise the potential profile close to the sheath region of an emissive wall or probe in the presence of dust particles. Additionally, to determine the wall temperature at which a virtual cathode forms in a dusty plasma.

- To study the interaction of charged dust particles in magnetized dusty plasma through scattering cross-section. A unique mathematical model incorporating a magnetic field is proposed and validated by means of COMSOL simulation.

- To investigate the dust acoustic instability (DAI) in a strongly coupled dusty plasma with a magnetic field. A novel mathematical analysis of the kinetic regime for strongly coupled dusty plasma with magnetic field is proposed for the growth analysis of DAI.

The thesis is organized as follows.

Chapter 2 Experimental Setup, diagnostics, and plasma characterization: This chapter discuss about the experimental setup of DPEx-II dusty plasma device and three probe diagnostics used i.e., Langmuir probe, Emissive probe and double Langmuir probe. A detailed description of the asymmetrical design of electrode is given in DC discharges. Three probe diagnostics are briefly explained with the design and operational aspects with the I-V curve. Various data points are collected in axial and radial direction through the probes and the results are plotted with various discharge voltage and pressure.

Chapter 3 Potential profile of virtual cathode in dusty plasma: This chapter describes the novel work of virtual cathode formation near an emissive wall in presence of dust particles with a mathematical treatment. A numerical method has been developed to observe virtual cathode near emissive wall/probe through sheath potential in presence of dust particles. Through phase space plot, an equilibrium points were identified for the formation of virtual cathode for different emission of electrons from the wall. It was learnt that virtual cathode indeed formed near emissive wall/probe in dusty plasma, but at higher emissive wall temperature in comparison to the absence of dust particles in plasma.

Chapter 4 Scattering cross-section of charged dust particles in magnetized dusty plasma: This chapter describe the interaction of charged dust particles with increasing magnetic field. A novel mathematical model is developed for description of charged dust particles in presence of **B**. From Coulomb scattering theory, scattering parameter is derived and plotted with respect to **B**. To justify the mathematical treatment, a lab identical DC plasma setup is designed in COMSOL simulation software and charged dust particles motion is tracked with varying B. In both numerical and computational treatment of the stated problem, it is observed that as B increases scattering cross-section of charged particle decreases and further the formation of coulomb crystals observed in simulation at increasing B. Both the results complimented each other, thus verifying the mathematical treatment of charged dust particles. Additionally, these results are compared with the previously performed experimental works.

Chapter 5 Dust acoustic instability: A quantitative analysis in presence of magnetic field: Dust acoustic instability (DAI) is studied in a strongly coupled dusty plasma system. The growth of the dust acoustic waves (DAW) is studied with Coulomb crystallization and in presence of magnetic field. Quasilocalized Charge Approximation (QLCA) method is implemented (kinetic regime) to calculate the dispersion relation and susceptibility of charge species. Most of the works has been in fluid regime or with fluid equations, hence QLCA method is compared with the fluid regime.

Chapter 6 Summary and Future scope of Works: This chapter provides the concluding remark and major output of the dissertation. Formation of dust crystals and DAW are analyzed through mathematical model in magnetized dusty plasma. It is also presented the future scopes and extension of the present work is discussed.

REFERENCES

1. Langmuir, I., Found, C. G., & Dittmer, A. F. (1924). A new type of electric discharge: The streamer discharge. *Science, 60*(1557), 392–394.
2. Alfvén, H. (1982). The origin of the solar system. In *Evolution in the Universe* (p. 31).
3. Spitzer, Jr., L. (1979). Physical processes in the interstellar medium (Book Review). *Astrophysical Letters, 20*, 57.
4. Selwyn, G. S., Singh, J., & Bennett, R. S. (1989). In situ laser diagnostic studies of plasma-generated particulate contamination. *Journal of Vacuum Science and Technology A, 7*(4), 2758–2765.
5. Selwyn, G. S., Heidenreich, J. E., & Haller, K. L. (1991). Rastered laser light scattering studies during plasma processing: Particle contamination trapping phenomena. *Journal of Vacuum Science and Technology A, 9*(5), 2817–2824.
6. Smith, B. A., Soderblom, L., Batson, R., Bridges, P., Inge, J. A. Y., Masursky, H., Shoemaker, E., Beebe, R., Boyce, J., Briggs, G., Bunker, A., Collins, S. A., Hansen, C. J., Johnson, T. V., Mitchell, J. L., Terrile, R. J., Cook, A. F., Cuzzi, J., Pollack, J. B., ... Suomi, V. E. (1982). A new look at the Saturn system: The Voyager 2 images. *Science, 215*(4532), 504–537.
7. Hill, J. R., & Mendis, D. A. (1980). Charged dust in the outer planetary magnetospheres. II-Trajectories and spatial distribution. *Moon and the Planets, 23*(1), 53–71.
8. Goertz, C. K., & Morfill, G. (1983). A model for the formation of spokes in Saturn's ring. *Icarus, 53*(2), 219–229.

9. Goertz, C. K. (1989). Dusty plasmas in the solar system. *Reviews of Geophysics, 27*(2), 271–292.
10. Narihara, K., Toi, K., Hamada, Y., Yamauchi, K., Adachi, K., Yamada, I., Sato, K. N., Kawahata, K., Nishizawa, A., Ohdachi, S., Sato, K., Seki, T., Watari, T., Xu, J., Ejiri, A., Hirokura, S., Ida, K., Kawasumi, Y., Kojima, M,. . & Kuramotyo, H. (1997). Observation of dust particles by a laser scattering method in the JIPPT-IIU Tokamak. *Nuclear Fusion, 37*(8), 1177–1182.
11. Winter, J. (2000). Dust: A new challenge in nuclear fusion research? *Physics of Plasmas, 7*(10), 3862–3866.
12. Krasheninnikov, S. I., Tomita, Y., Smirnov, R. D., & Janev, R. K. (2004). On dust dynamics in Tokamak edge plasmas. *Physics of Plasmas, 11*(6), 3141–3150.
13. Krasheninnikov, S., Smolyakov, A., & Kukushkin, A. (2020). *On the edge of magnetic fusion devices*. Springer International Publishing.
14. Chen, F. F. (2012). *Introduction to plasma physics*. Springer Science & Business Media.
15. Feng, Y., Goree, J., & Liu, B. (2007). Accurate particle position measurement from images. *Review of Scientific Instruments, 78*(5), 053704.
16. Thomas, Jr., E. (1999). Direct measurements of two-dimensional velocity profiles in direct current glow discharge dusty plasmas. *Physics of Plasmas, 6*(7), 2672–2675.
17. Shukla, P. K., & Mamun, A. A. (2015). *Introduction to dusty plasma physics*. CRC Press.
18. Bonitz, M., Horing, N., & Ludwig, P. (Eds.). (2010). *Introduction to complex plasmas, 59*. Springer Science & Business Media.
19. Melzer, A. (2019). *Physics of dusty plasmas*. Springer International Publishing.
20. Chen, F. F. (1965) Plasma Diagnostic Techniques R. H. Huddlestone & S. L. Leonard (Eds.). Academic Press Chapter 4.

21. Allen, J. E. (1992). Probe theory-the orbital motion approach. *Physica Scripta, 45*(5), 497–503.
22. Barkan, A., D'Angelo, N., & Merlino, R. L. (1994). Charging of dust grains in a plasma. *Physical Review Letters, 73*(23), 3093–3096.
23. Chu, J. H., & I, L. (1994). Direct observation of Coulomb crystals and liquids in strongly coupled rf dusty plasmas. *Physical Review Letters, 72*(25), 4009–4012.
24. Fortov, V. E., Molotkov, V. I., Nefedov, A. P., & Petrov, O. F. (1999). Liquid-and crystallike structures in strongly coupled dusty plasmas. *Physics of Plasmas, 6*(5), 1759–1768.
25. Thomas, H., Morfill, G. E., Demmel, V., Goree, J., Feuerbacher, B., & Möhlmann, D. (1994). Plasma crystal: Coulomb crystallization in a dusty plasma. *Physical Review Letters, 73*(5), 652–655.
26. Chu, J. H., & I, L. (1994). Coulomb lattice in a weakly ionized colloidal plasma. *Physica A: Statistical Mechanics and its Applications, 205*(1–3), 183–190.
27. Barnes, M. S., Keller, J. H., Forster, J. C., O'Neill, J. A., & Coultas, D. K. (1992). Transport of dust particles in glow-discharge plasmas. *Physical Review Letters, 68*(3), 313–316.
28. Bittencourt, J. A. (2004). *Fundamentals of plasma physics*. Springer Science & Business Media.
29. Nitter, T. (1996). Levitation of dust in rf and d.c. glow discharges. *Plasma Sources Science and Technology, 5*(1), 93–111.
30. Epstein, P. S. (1924). On the resistance experienced by spheres in their motion through gases. *Physical Review, 23*(6), 710–733.
31. Talbot, L., Cheng, R. K., Schefer, R. W., & Willis, D. R. (1980) Thermophoresis of particles in a heated boundary layer. *Journal of Fluid Mechanics, 101*(4), 737–758.

32. Daugherty, J. E., & Graves, D. B. (1995). Derivation and experimental verification of a particulate transport model for a glow discharge. *Journal of Applied Physics, 78*(4), 2279–2287.
33. Ikezi, H. (1986). Coulomb solid of small particles in plasmas. *Physics of Fluids, 29*(6), 1764–1766.
34. Nakamura, Y., & Bailung, H. (1999). A dusty double plasma device. *Review of Scientific Instruments, 70*(5), 2345–2348.
35. Piel, A. (2010). *Plasma physics: An introduction to laboratory, space, and fusion plasmas*. Springer.
36. Bellan, P. M. (2004). A model for the condensation of a dusty plasma. *Physics of Plasmas, 11*(7), 3368–3379.
37. Barkan, A., D'Angelo, N., & Merlino, R. L. (1994). Charging of dust grains in a plasma. *Physical Review Letters, 73*(23), 3093–3096.
38. Thomas, E., Merlino, R. L., & Rosenberg, M. (2012). Magnetized dusty plasmas: The next frontier for complex plasma research. *Plasma Physics and Controlled Fusion, 54*(12), 124034.
39. Kählert, H., Melzer, A., Puttscher, M., Ott, T., & Bonitz, M. (2018). Magnetic field effects and waves in complex plasmas. *European Physical Journal D, 72*(5), 1–8.
40. Nosenko, V., Goree, J., Ma, Z. W., Dubin, D. H. E., & Piel, A. (2003). Compressional and shear wakes in a two-dimensional dusty plasma crystal. *Physical Review E, 68*(5), 056409.
41. Couëdel, L., Nosenko, V., Ivlev, A. V., Zhdanov, S. K., Thomas, H. M., & Morfill, G. E. (2010). Direct observation of mode-coupling instability in two-dimensional plasma crystals. *Physical Review Letters, 104*(19), 195001.
42. Bailung, Y., Deka, T., Boruah, A., Sharma, S. K., Pal, A. R., Chutia, J., & Bailung, H. (2018). Characteristics of dust voids in a strongly coupled laboratory dusty plasma. *Physics of Plasmas, 25*(5), 053705.

43. Fedoseev, A. V., Sukhinin, G. I., Abdirakhmanov, A. R., Dosbolayev, M. K., & Ramazanov, T. S. (2016). Voids in dusty plasma of a stratified DC glow discharge in noble gases. *Contributions to Plasma Physics, 56*(3–4), 234–239.
44. Fedoseev, A. V., Sukhinin, G. I., Dosbolayev, M. K., & Ramazanov, T. S. (2015). Dust-void formation in a d.c. glow discharge. *Physical Review E, 92*(2), 023106.
45. Bastykova, N. Kh., Kovács, A. Zs., Korolov, I., Kodanova, S. K., Ramazanov, T. S., Hartmann, P., & Donkó, Z. (2015). Controlled levitation of dust particles in RF & DC discharges. *Contributions to Plasma Physics, 55*(9), 671–676.
46. Thomas, Jr., E., Amatucci, W. E., & Morfill, G. E. (2002). Boundary phenomena in RF and DC glow discharge dusty plasmas. *In AIP Conference Proceedings*. American Institute of Physics, *649*(1), 243–246.
47. Nitter, T. (1996). Levitation of dust in rf and d.c. glow discharges. *Plasma Sources Science and Technology, 5*(1), 93–111.
48. Piel, A., & Melzer, A. (2002). Dusty plasmas-the state of understanding from an experimentalist's view. *Advances in Space Research, 29*(9), 1255–1264.
49. Jaiswal, S., Bandyopadhyay, P., & Sen, A. (2015). Dusty plasma experimental (dpex) device for complex plasma experiments with flow. *Review of Scientific Instruments, 86*(11), 113503.
50. Langmuir, I. (1929). The interaction of electron and positive ion space charges in cathode sheaths. *Physical Review, 33*(6), 954–989.
51. Tonks, L., & Langmuir, I. (1929). A general theory of the plasma of an arc. *Physical Review, 34*(6), 876–922.
52. Hobbs, G. D., & Wesson, J. A. (1967). Heat flow through a Langmuir sheath in the presence of electron emission. *Plasma Physics, 9*(1), 85–87.

53. Intrator, T., Cho, M. H., Wang, E. Y., Hershkowitz, N., Diebold, D., & DeKock, J. (1988). The virtual cathode as a transient double sheath. *Journal of Applied Physics, 64*(6), 2927–2933.
54. Gyergyek, T., Jurčič-Zlobec, B., Čerček, M., & Kovačič, J. (2009). Sheath structure in front of an electron emitting electrode immersed in a two-electron temperature plasma: A fluid model and numerical solutions of the Poisson equation. *Plasma Sources Science and Technology, 18*(3), 035001.
55. Ye, M. Y., & Takamura, S. (2000). Effect of space-charge limited emission on measurements of plasma potential using emissive probes. *Physics of Plasmas, 7*(8), 3457–3463.
56. Sheehan, J. P., Hershkowitz, N., Kaganovich, I. D., Wang, H., Raitses, Y., Barnat, E. V., Weatherford, B. R., & Sydorenko, D. (2013). Kinetic theory of plasma sheaths surrounding electron-emitting surfaces. *Physical Review Letters, 111*(7), 075002.
57. Merlino, R. L. (2014). 25 years of dust acoustic waves. *Journal of Plasma Physics, 80*(6), 773–786.
58. Mamun, A. A., & Shukla, P. K. (2011). Discoveries of waves in dusty plasmas. *Journal of Plasma Physics, 77*(4), 437–455.
59. Rao, N. N., Shukla, P. K., & Yu, M. Y. (1990). Dust-acoustic waves in dusty plasmas. *Planetary and Space Science, 38*(4), 543–546.
60. Barkan, A., D'Angelo, N., & Merlino, R. L. (1995). Laboratory experiments on electrostatic ion cyclotron waves in a dusty plasma. *Planetary and Space Science, 43*(7), 905–908.
61. Verheest, F. (2000). *Waves in dusty space plasmas*, 245. Springer Science & Business Media.
62. Li, F., Havnes, O., & Melandsø, F. (1994). Longitudinal waves in a dusty plasma. *Planetary and Space Science, 42*(5), 401–407.
63. D'Angelo, N. (1990). Low-frequency electrostatic waves in dusty plasmas. *Planetary and Space Science, 38*(9), 1143–1146.

64. Bharuthram, R., & Shukla, P. K. (1992). Large amplitude ion-acoustic solitons in a dusty plasma. *Planetary and Space Science, 40*(7), 973–977.
65. Nakamura, Y., & Sarma, A. (2001). Observation of ion-acoustic solitary waves in a dusty plasma. *Physics of Plasmas, 8*(9), 3921–3926.

CHAPTER 2

EXPERIMENTAL SETUP, DIAGNOSTICS AND PLASMA CHARACTERIZATION

2.1 INTRODUCTION

The complete experimental works have been carried out for this thesis is on the Dusty Plasma Experimental (DPEx-II) setup built up at Institute of Plasma Research (IPR), which hosts the facility for performing experiments such as dust flow, dust crystals, solitons, phase transitions etc. The main objective of the device is to study dust particle crystallization and phase transition. Therefore, the design of the instrument has been influenced by the DPEx-I device that studies the flow of dust particles in plasma with various grid potentials [1-5]. However, the length and diameter of vacuum chamber and size of the electrodes are different in DPEx-II setup. Dimension and design of the experimental setup are discussed in section 2.2. This section also discusses the need for such design of experimental setups for the variety of experiments to be carried out in near future. Section 2.3 discusses the probe diagnostic tool used for measurement of plasma characterization of DPEx-II. Different types of probe measurement, design and characterization are explained in this section. This chapter also includes the brief elaboration of probe diagnostics and design of probes used for characterization of plasma in experimental setup. Plasma characterization of DPEx-II setup through the length and breadth of vacuum chamber is presented graphically in section 2.4. Section 2.5 is comprising of brief discussion of DPEx-II setup with plasma parameters such as plasma density, electron temperature etc.

2.2 EXPERIMENTAL SETUP

Experimental setup of Dusty Plasma Experimental (DPEx-II) consist of vacuum chamber, power supply systems, electrodes etc., and are discussed about physical and technical details in subsequent sections.

2.2.1 VACUUM CHAMBER AND ELECTRODE CONFIGURATIONS

DPEx-II is mounted on a tabletop setup with a vacuum chamber of length 60 cm and inner diameter of 15 cm. Vacuum chamber is made of Pyrex glass to observe visibly the flow of dust particles through CCD Camera and record the observation though images. Experimental setups consist of various ports i.e., radially and axially on the vacuum chamber as can be seen from Fig. 2.1. Along the ports attached are rotary pump, probes, gas injection (MFC - mass flow controller) etc. MFC is used for control of flow of the gas into the vacuum chamber. L shaped design is inspired from the well-documented and characterized DPEx-I setup. The design of electrodes in DPEx-II is unconventional and asymmetric which has its own benefits for studies of charge dust particles and its associated properties. The anode is positioned 10 cm above the cathode through a vertical tube with a length of 58 cm and an ID of 10 cm. The anode is a circular Stainless Steel (SS) disc with a diameter of 5 cm. The cathode is a long, elongated rectangular stainless-steel tray that runs the length of the vacuum chamber. The cathode is grounded and has dimension of 40 cm × 15 cm × 2 mm, which is very large area compared to the anode area. In most of the plasma electrode discharge experimental configurations, electrodes are kept same size and parallel to each other, thus flux of electrons towards anode and flux of ions towards cathode will be same. Contrarily, in asymmetric electrode configurations like in DPEx-II setup, anode is kept small compared to the cathode, such that flux of electrons and ions will be different at respective electrodes. Cathode with a larger area reduces considerably the ion flux, and ions entering the cathode sheath with lower velocity. Therefore, reducing the impact of momentum on dust particles and reducing the ion heating effect on dust particles [6].

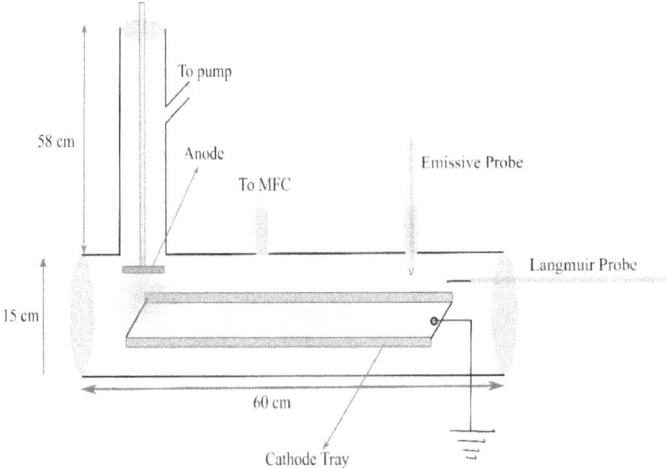

Fig. 2.1. Schematic diagram of DPEx-II device with probe diagnostics

Keeping this in mind, the idea of having asymmetric electrode configuration in DPEx-II setup has been considered. Additionally, the edges of the cathode have been folded up to height of 2 cm along the length of the cathode tray as shown in Fig. 2.1. Folded edges of the cathode tray enable the flux of ions moving away from the center of the tray and streaming towards the edges. This fact can be observed after long exposure of cathode in plasma and burnt surfaces were noticed due to ion bombardment on edges [7].

2.2.2 POWER SUPPLY AND PUMPING SYSTEMS

To begin, a rotary pump linked to one of the ports in a vertical tube is used to empty the vacuum chamber to a base pressure of 10^{-3} mbar. Two Pirani gauges, one in a vertical tube and the other above the horizontal chamber are kept to, measure and monitor the pressure in the chamber. A controlled amount of Ar gas is fed through MFC in one of the ports of the horizontal chamber. Preliminary, the vacuum chamber is flushed out with any external gas or background contamination present through rotary pump and finally chamber is filled with Ar in controlled amount of working pressure 0.1 mbar to 0.14 mbar. A Direct Current (DC) power supply (0 to 1 kV) is used for producing the plasma in chamber. A current limiting resistor of 2 kΩ is connected between power supply and anode for further safety of power supply. Voltage of 275 V to 400 V is applied to the anode for plasma generation in chamber.

2.3 PROBE DIAGNOSTICS

Electrostatic diagnostics has been one of the fundamental ways of measuring or quantifying plasma. Irving Langmuir (1929) demonstrated that a metallic wire inserted in the plasma collects the electron and ion currents from the plasma, and plasma parameters are measured with respect to bias voltage. Due to the collective behavior of plasma, a local perturbation or oscillation gives an approximation of behavior of plasma particles (electrons and ions). Electron temperature, electron and ion density, plasma potential and floating potential are some of the basic parameters that can be determined from the probe. These parameters are measured from the Current-Voltage (I-V) curve that is plotted by biasing the probe with voltage source. Mostly used electric probes in any plasma diagnostics are Langmuir probe, double Langmuir Probe, Triple Langmuir Probe, Ion energy analyzer and Emissive probe. Optical and spectroscopic techniques are the few diagnostics used without probing or remotely monitoring plasma. There are three electrostatic diagnostics that are used in the DPEx-II setup namely Langmuir Probe, Emissive Probe, and double Langmuir Probe. Discussion of each probe is given in subsequent sections such as theory, design, and measurements.

2.3.1 LANGMUIR PROBE

Langmuir probe is a metallic wire connected through bias voltage and measuring the flux of currents arriving at the wire with different biased voltage. For many decades, single Langmuir probe is used for estimation of plasma parameters. A metallic wire is usually made of a material with a high melting point and is insulated by a ceramic holder as shown in Fig. 2.2 (a) and (b), respectively. Tungsten is used as the metallic wire in this experiment.

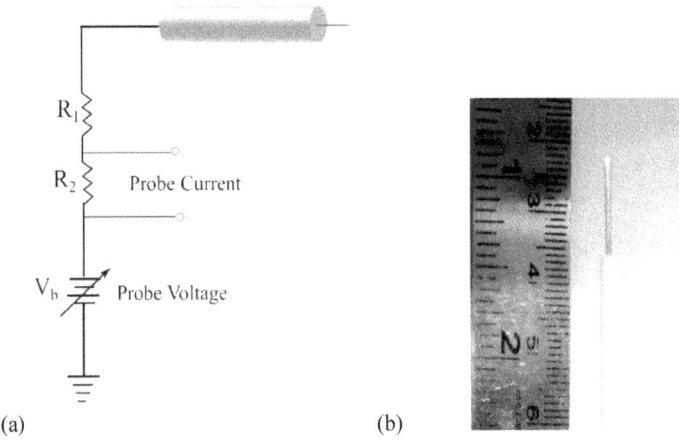

Fig. 2.2 (a) Schematic diagram of Langmuir Probe circuit. (b) Tungsten Probe with ceramic holder

A tungsten wire of length 10 mm and 1 mm in diameter is probed into plasma with ceramic holder as an insulating material as shown in Fig. 2.2(b). The probe part that is required for collection of signals in the form of currents from plasma is only exposed and rest is insulated. The probe dimension must be fixed in such a way that it does not disrupt the plasma equilibrium. If the probe is sufficient small, then probe can melt or break in plasma. Hence, it becomes necessary to have the right dimension of probe. In addition, through BNC cable, probe is biased through probe power supply and output is taken from oscilloscope as in I-V curve.

Schematic diagram of probe biasing circuit is shown in Fig. 2.2 (a). For starter, floating potential is measured through the high value resistor connected in series such that a bias voltage to the probe i.e., ramp voltage is determined. Floating potential, (V_f) is the potential at which current collected by the probe is zero i.e., the net flux of ion and electron reaching the probe surface is same. The equal number of currents (electrons and ions) from plasma on the probe is zero. If bias voltage (V_b) to the probe is applied higher than V_f, then the probe gathers the electron current from the plasma. If $V_b < V_f$, then probe collects ions currents from plasma. An ideal I-V curve is shown in Fig. 2.3. The current collected from the probe is drawn with applied bias voltage. This is the typical characteristics I-V curve of Langmuir Probe measurements. The methods to extract the data from I-V curve was given by Chen (1989).

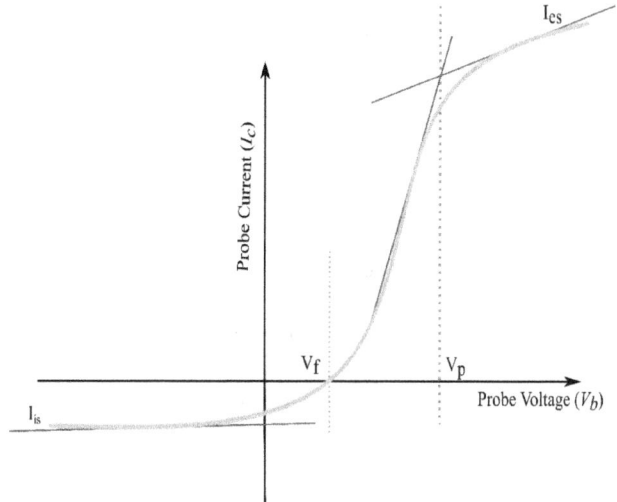

Fig. 2.3. An ideal I-V plot from the Langmuir probe in plasma.

With the help of MATLAB, ion saturation current (I_{is}), electron saturation current (I_{es}), floating potential (V_f), and plasma potential (V_p) have been determined. Let us discuss about the characterization parameter of plasma through IV curve plotted as given in Fig. 2.3. For $V_f > V_b$, ion currents are collected on the probe. The flat line exhibits ion saturation current for highly negative V_b w.r.t V_f and can be determined from

$$I_{is} = 0.6\, q n_i v_{bohm} A_{probe} \qquad (2.1)$$

where q is the charge, A_{probe} is probe collection area, n_i is ion density and v_{Bohm} is Bohm velocity given by $\sqrt{8 k_B T_e / m_i}$ such that the ion mass is m_i, k_B is Boltzmann's constant and T_e is electron temperature, respectively. For a negatively biased probe, the ions should reach the positive sheath region with a velocity greater than of Bohm velocity (v_{Bohm}) [6]. Further, to achieve this velocity ion should reach same as T_e. Numerical value of 0.6 is due to the factor of pre-sheath region where ions are accelerated up to Bohm speed [6]. For $V_p > V_b > V_f$, this region is called as transition region where both electrons and ions are collected on the probe from plasma and give the information about the energy of electrons. For $V_b > V_p$, majority of the particle reaching the probe is electrons. V_p is a plasma potential at which random currents of electrons and ions are observed on probe. If V_b is increased more positively than V_p, sheath region around the probe starts to diminish and electron currents to the probe gets saturated as shown in Fig. 2.3. This is called the electron saturation current (I_{es}) and maximum current collected by probe is given by

$$I_{es} = (1/4) q n_e V_{Te} A_{probe} \qquad (2.2)$$

where V_{Te} is electron thermal speed given as $\sqrt{8 k_B T_e / \pi m_e}$ and m_e is the electron mass.

2.3.2 EMISSIVE PROBE

The plasma potential or space potential (V_p) is particularly important parameter in terms of determining the plasma properties such as confinement or charge particle (electrons and ions) flows [8-12]. However, experimental measurement of V_p through Langmuir Probe is not accurate as probe draws currents which influences plasma particles indirectly. Further, error in measurement occurs when there is layer of coatings on probes by plasma ions. Again, if there is a temperature fluctuation and a non-steady state of plasma, Langmuir probes cannot be used. Hence, emissive, or hot probes are used for being simple in practical implementation and measurements with less uncertainty [13-15]. Langmuir was the first to implement an electron-emitting probe in 1923, at the same time as he proposed the idea of collecting probes (Langmuir Probes) [16]. Plasma potential can be measured precisely by a $T_e/10q$ for high signal to noise ratio. A typical design structure of emissive probe and probe used in experiments is shown in Fig. 2.4. Filament is enclosed by an insulating material in a ceramic tube connecting to the Cu leads, which is connected to the current source. Electrons are emitted from the filament with increasing current. Moreover, emitted electron temperature (T_w) is always less than the T_e, such that plasma potential measurement becomes more accurate [17].

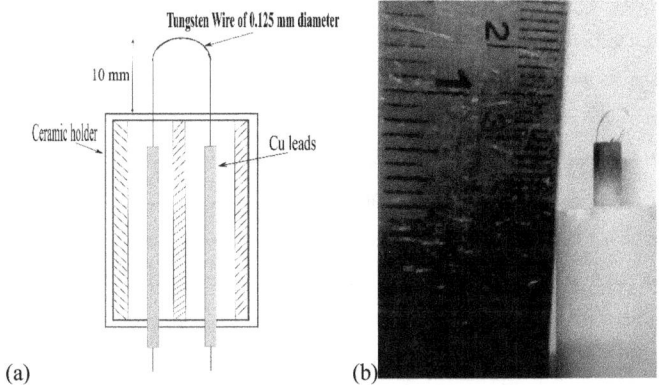

Fig. 2.4. (a) Hairpin structure of emissive probe (b) Real design structure of tungsten filament of 0.125 mm diameter and 10 mm length.

In low-temperature plasmas, a thin layer of charges called 'sheath' is formed near the plasma-exposed surface and is always negatively charged with respect to the plasma due to the fast electrons, which are much lighter than heavier ions. As a result, the sheath's negative electric field prevents more electron currents from reaching the probe. The negative charge on the probe is reduced when electrons are emitted from the emissive probe. Consequently, there is a decrease in voltage drop in the plasma-sheath interface as emission increases. Therefore, the technique of floating the electron-emitting probe at a plasma potential is the basic principle used in measurement of plasma potential in emissive probe diagnostics. Further, probe can be biased with an electrical circuit in relation to reference potential. Both floating and biased emissive probes do not provide precise plasma potential measurements, with the former being less accurate than the latter. However, floating emissive probes can be still used in harsh environments of plasmas such as plasma thrusters, gas exhausts, spacecraft etc. where probes can be kept for a second or less. On the other hand, dependence of biasing the probe with respect to plasma potential influences emission of electrons from the probe surface. If probe is biased highly negative than the plasma potential, then electrons are emitted from the probe surface into the plasma. Electric field in the sheath accelerates the electrons from surface to the plasma. If probe is biased highly positive than the plasma potential, then electrons are not emitted from the probe except only for highly energetic electrons. This can be seen from the Fig. 2.5 where $V_p = 0$ and $T_e = 1.0$ eV [18]. As probe bias voltage (V_b) is increased above V_p, there is no emission of electrons. Whereas, for $V_b < V_p$, constant emission of current is observed. This is sometimes called temperature limited electron emission because filament's temperature limits the electrons emission. A more rigorous theory is presented for floating and biased emissive probes [8, 17-19]. Equations which describe the theoretical curve of I-V for Fig. 2.5 is given by both collected and emitted currents as

$$I_e(V_b) = \begin{cases} I_e^* exp\left(\frac{-e(V_p-V_b)}{T_e}\right), & V_b \leq V_p \\ I_e^* g_e(V_b - V_p), & V_b > V_p \end{cases} \quad (2.3)$$

$$I_{em}(V_b) = \begin{cases} I_{et}, & V_b < V_p \\ I_{et} \exp\left(\frac{-e(V_p - V_b)}{T_{em}}\right) g_{em}(V_b - V_p), & V_b \geq V_p \end{cases} \quad (2.4)$$

where $g_e(V_b - V_p)$ and $g_{em}(V_b - V_p)$ is the angular momentum of collected and emitted electrons; I_{et} is the thermionic emission current given by Richardson-Dushman equation [20] and electron saturation current; and T_{em} is thermionic emitted electron temperature. A more detailed derivation of the equations can be seen in [21].

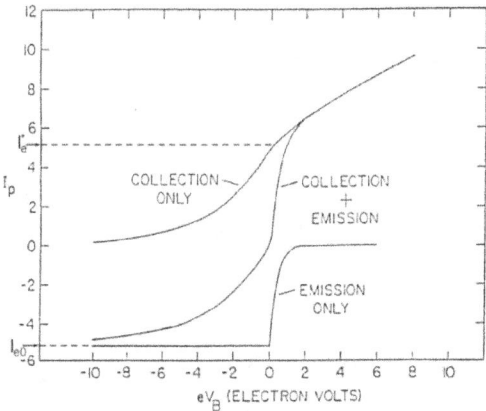

Fig. 2.5. Theoretical I-V curve of an emissive probe. (Image Credit: Hershkowitz (1989) [17])

However, there is one aspect of hindrance in measurement of plasma potential through emission of electrons from the probe is space charge effects. This is the result of imbalance of fluxes collected on the probe to the emission of electrons from probe. Additionally, difference between electron temperature collected and emitted electron temperature (T_{em}) plays a major role in potential drop of plasma sheath. Therefore, only T_e affects the sheath potential decrease in space-charge-limited emission [8, 22];

$$\phi_{sheath} \approx -\frac{T_e}{e} \quad (2.5)$$

When emission of electrons is increased from probe by increasing current through filament, accumulation of negative charges is observed near probe. Thus, creating a negative well of emitted electrons near probe in the sheath called as Virtual cathode. After formation of virtual cathode, only few emitted electrons escape the sheath, thus potential in the sheath drops more negative. This phenomenon effects the measurement of plasma potential, as the difference between floating and plasma potential increases. Space charge effects is not included in the theory of emissive probe. Ye and Takamura were the first one to describe the space charge effects analytically [23].

2.3.2.1 METHODS OF DETERMINING PLASMA POTENTIAL FROM EMISSIVE PROBE

Plasma potential through emissive probe can be determined by three different techniques: (i) Separation point method, (ii) floating point method and (iii) inflection point method. In detailed discussion of these techniques are presented in this section.

Separation Point Method: One of the basic assumptions in this method is to emit the electrons from the probe below plasma potential. The emission should maintain in such a way that the modulus of ion and electron collection current is almost same. Hence, emitted electrons have almost zero energy and space charge effects are neglected [16]. I-V curves of cold probe i.e., no emission of electrons and hot probe i.e., emission of electrons are drawn together such that to see where these two curves diverge. Therefore, the point at which these two curves diverge is a measure of plasma potential [24, 25]. However, space charge effects will be dominating in electron emission from probe such that a deviation of I-V curve brings error in measurement of plasma potential. Due to this factor, there is doubt in measurement of plasma potential in separation point technique.

Floating Point Method: This technique is the most popular for the measurement of plasma potential firstly given by Kemp and Sellen [26]. This method involves measuring the plasma potential through saturation of floating potential. At first, probe is kept as floating in plasma such that flux of electrons and ions becomes zero at the probe. This floating potential is recorded and progressively with increase in emission of electrons from probe floating potential is measured. Initially V_f increases with increase in emission, and later at some higher emission, V_f goes saturating. This V_f saturation point is the measure of plasma potential. This technique is quick and easy to measure the V_p as it evolves with spatial and temporal. However, space charge effects cause measurement error where V_f saturates below the V_p of the order T_e/q. If T_e is small, then there are small deviations from the measurement of V_p. If T_e is very large, then there is a significant difference in measurement of V_p and becomes inaccurate. Even so, this technique is widely used and even in measurement of V_p in fusion plasma.

Inflection Point Method: To reduce the space charge effects, Smith *et al.* (1979) developed a method related to V_f[19]. I-V curve is drawn for lower limit of zero emission as shown in Fig. 2.6. Inflection point exists at the plasma potential for cold probe but as soon as emission increases inflection point becomes negative. Inflection point is determined by taking derivative of I-V curve and identifying the peak point. The inflection point values are plotted with temperature limited emission, and linear extrapolation to zero emission yields the inflection point in the limit of zero emission plasma potential measure. Despite of measuring V_p accurately, inflection point method is not suitable technique for every experiment such as at high density plasma, and large temporal variations. Furthermore, if the electron temperature is low, the disparity between the floating point and inflection point methods can be minimized. Error in measurement of floating-point method can remain constant if T_e is constant and hence measurement of V_p will still be correct.

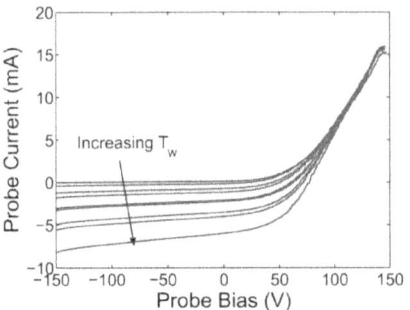

Fig. 2.6. In the limit of zero emission method, I-V traces are drawn with increasing emission. (Image Credit: Sheehan *et al.* (2011) [27])

These both methods i.e., floating-point method and separation point method have been employed in this dissertation.

2.3.3 DOUBLE LANGMUIR PROBE

Double Langmuir probe is a two single Langmuir probes separated by a distance (mostly greater than Debye length) [28]. Single Langmuir probe always takes the vessel reference or electrode reference for measurements making directly contact to bulk plasma. Thus, single Langmuir probe has limitations of usage in dielectric chamber and electrodeless discharges. Secondly, single Langmuir probe draws large current from the bulk plasma for measurements. Conversely, double Langmuir probe doesn't require any reference electrode, nor it draws much current making less perturbations to the plasma. Double Langmuir probe generally measures the electric field in plasma, but in most of the time, it is used to measure the electron temperature and plasma density. In this dissertation work, double Langmuir probe is used to measure the electron temperature profile.

Double Langmuir probe uses two Tungsten wire of length 10 mm and diameter of 1 mm separated by a distance of 10 mm enclosed in a ceramic holder as shown in Fig. 2.7. From the measurements of single Langmuir probe,

Debye length has been estimated around 0.15 mm to 0.35 mm, which is much smaller than the separated distance between two wires in double Langmuir probe. The basic operation of double Langmuir probe can be understood from the electrical circuit diagram as shown in Fig. 2.7 (b). Both probes are biased with respect to each other. For plotting I-V curve, one probe is biased with -40 V to + 40 V with respect to another probe and current is measured through the 1 kΩ resistor. Potential of the probe 1 (P1) and probe 2 (P2) is taken as φ_1 and φ_2 such that

$$V = \varphi_1 - \varphi_2 \tag{2.6}$$

Electron currents to the P1 and P2 are given as I_{e1} and I_{e2}, whereas ion currents is given as I_{i1} and I_{i2}. Therefore, total current on the probe is given as [28]

$$I_p = I_{i1} - I_{e1} + I_{i2} - I_{e2} \tag{2.7}$$

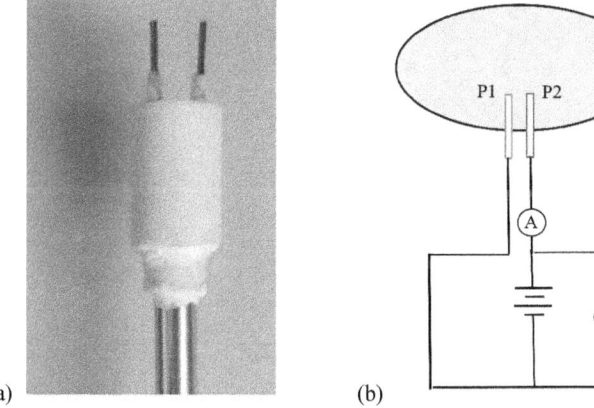

(a)   (b)

Fig. 2.7. (a) Double Langmuir probe (b) Circuit diagram of double Langmuir probe

Generally, current is from the two probes such as $I_p = I_{p1} + I_{p2}$, since equal number of currents are drawn from both probes I_p can be written as $2I$

$$2I = I_{i1} - I_{e1} + I_{i2} - I_{e2} \tag{2.8}$$

From Eqn (2.7) and (2.8), I can be written as

$$I = I_{i1} - I_{e1} = I_{i2} - I_{e2} \qquad (2.9)$$

where I_{e1} and I_{e2} is given as

$$I_{e1} = A_1 J_{e0} exp\left(\frac{-q\varphi_1}{T_e}\right) \qquad (2.10)$$

$$I_{e2} = A_2 J_{e0} exp\left(\frac{-q\varphi_2}{T_e}\right) \qquad (2.11)$$

J_{e0} is the equilibrium electron current density; A_1 & A_2 is the probe area of P1 and P2. Substituting Eqn. (2.10) & (2.11) in (2.9)

$$\frac{I + I_{i1}}{I_{i2} + I} = \frac{A_1}{A_2} exp\left(\frac{q\varphi_{vd}}{T_e}\right) \qquad (2.12)$$

where φ_{vd} is the voltage difference and $A_1 = A_2$ as both probes has equal size and area. Hence, $I_{i1} = I_{i2}$ and Eqn. (2.12) can be written as

$$I = I_{is} \tanh\left(\frac{q\varphi_{vd}}{T_e}\right) \qquad (2.13)$$

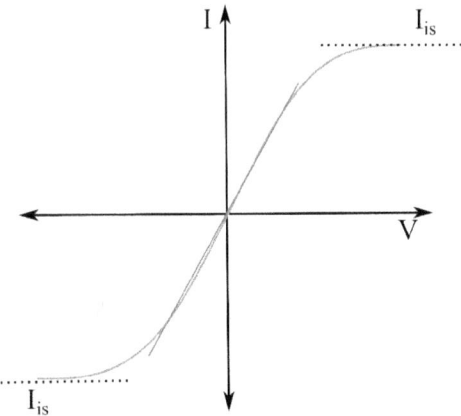

Fig. 2.8. Pictorial presentation of I-V characteristics of double Langmuir probe

The I-V characteristics curve of double Langmuir probe is shown in Fig. 2.8. From the figure, electron temperature (T_e) can be measured directly from the slope drawn at the center of the coordinate axis shown as green line on the curve.

2.4 PLASMA CHARACTERIZATION

All three probes were connected to oscilloscope through BNC cable and the data is collected on external pen drive attached to one of the ports on oscilloscope. A program is developed in MATLAB to find out the plasma parameters as explained in earlier sections. DC voltage is applied across the electrodes from 275 V to 375 V and vacuum pressure is varied between 0.1 mbar to 0.14 mbar for Ar gas. Base pressure of vacuum chamber is kept at 0.01 mbar. Fig. 2.9 shows the schematic view of DPEx-II device.

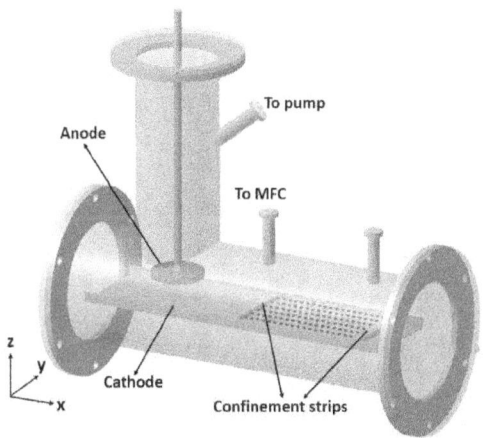

Fig. 2.9. Schematic 3D design of DPEx-II device.

The Langmuir probe is scanned across the cathode tray at a distance of just over 50 mm. Langmuir probe is biased through probe power supply ranging from 270 V to 320 V, which is above floating potential. Foremost, electron temperature is measured from I-V curve. Fig. 2.10 (a) and (b) shows the electron temperature (T_e) measurement from the probe for various voltage and pressure. It is observed that T_e varies from 1 eV to 3.5 eV throughout the length of the cathode tray. Due to the low pressure, and the asymmetry of electrodes, there was large fluctuations in measurement of parameters. Hence, large error bar indication in the measurements. As DC voltage or pressure increases, energy is transferred to the plasma species through inelastic scattering of electrons. Consequently, electron collision frequency increases with plasma species. Therefore, it is observed that T_e decreases with increase in voltage and pressure as shown in Fig. 2.10. However, there is not much large variation of T_e with increase in voltage and value remains same along the length of vacuum chamber.

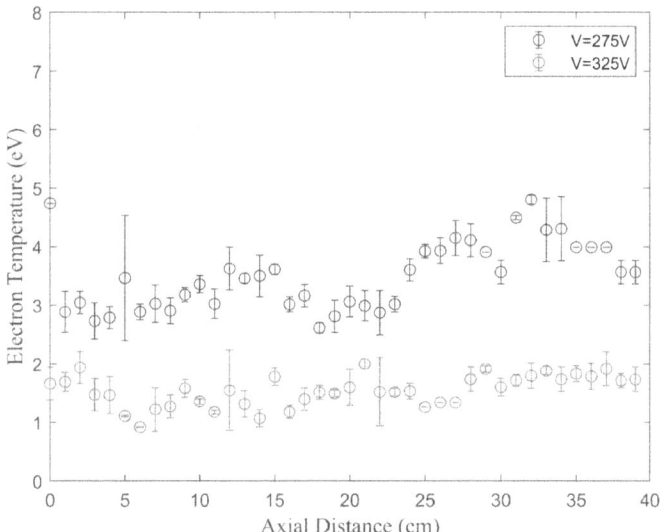

Fig. 2.10 T_e measured at constant pressure 0.12 mbar with varying voltage. Probe is scanned through the length of cathode tray, taking starting point near anode to farther end of the cathode.

With the increase in pressure or voltage, ionization increases inside the plasma chamber and further reducing the mean free path of the plasma particles (electrons and ions). Successive collisions result in decrease of T_e with increase in pressure. It is also observed that T_e is almost constant along the length of the vacuum chamber.

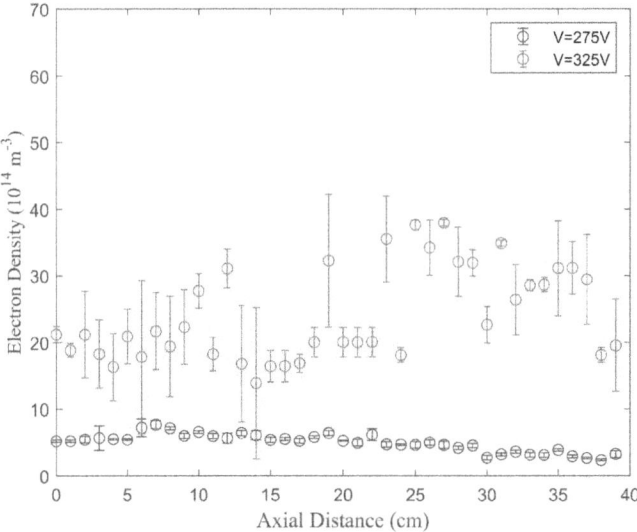

Fig. 2.11 (a) n_e with various DC voltage at constant pressure of 0.12 mbar. Probe is measured along the length of vacuum chamber above the cathode tray.

Plasma density has been obtained from the theoretical calculation of MATLAB as shown in Fig. 2.11. From Eqn. (2.2), it is known that there is an inverse relationship between T_e and electron density (n_e). As T_e decreasing with increase in voltage or pressure as shown in Fig. 2.10, the electron density increases as shown in Fig. 2.11 (a) & (b). It is due to fact that, rate of collisions between electrons and neutrals increases. Fig. 2.11 (a) shows the n_e variation with increase in voltage with constant pressure of 0.12 mbar. Fig. 2.11 (b) show the n_e variation with increase in pressure at constant voltage of 325 V. There is not much difference of n_e with increase in pressure due to the very less difference of pressure. Additionally, it can be observed that, n_e remains constant along the length of chamber.

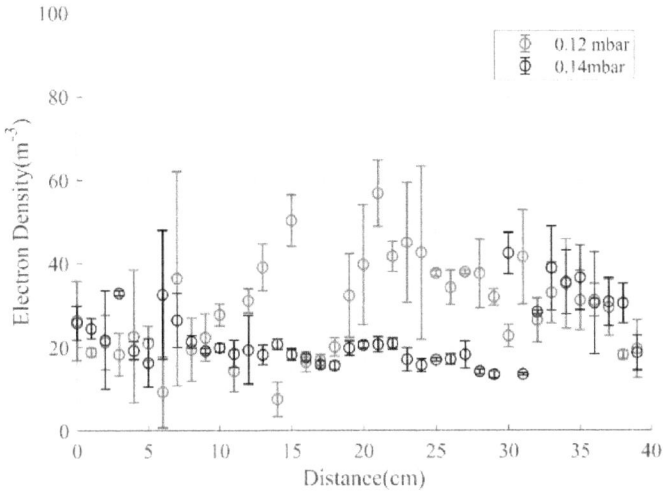

Fig. 2.11(b) n_e with increase in gas pressure at constant V = 325 V

Floating potential and plasma potential is measured from the probe I-V curve as shown in Fig. 2.12 (a) and (b). The increase of V_p and V_f at particular position due to the increase in DC voltage can be attributed to the presence of energetic electrons. V_f ranges from 280 V to 310 V and V_p ranges from 290 V to 320 V. Both V_f and V_p remains same along the length of the chamber with a difference of 5 to 10 V.

All the parameters have been measured and plotted from the Langmuir probe along the length of vacuum chamber. These measurements will be helpful in understanding the dynamics and studies of charge dust particles as mentioned in section 2.1. Although, due to large fluctuations in plasma chamber, recording the measurements had been difficult. In such cases, large fluctuations become problem in measurement of plasma parameters, then emissive probe becomes useful.

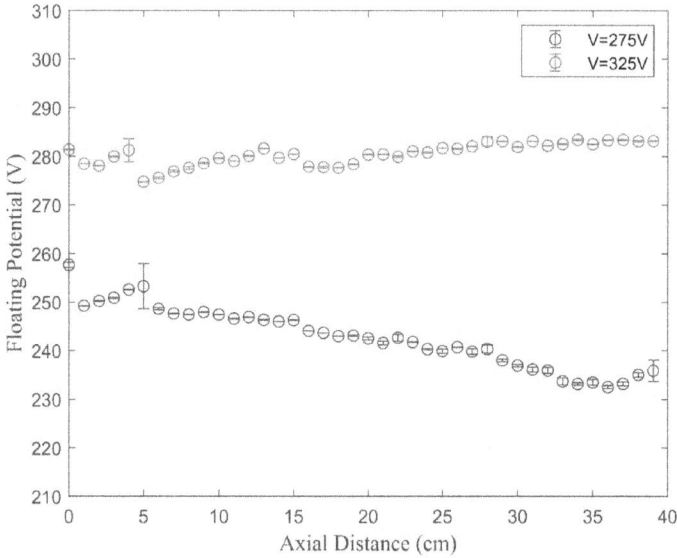

Fig. 2.12 (a) V_f at constant pressure of 0.12 mbar measured along the length of the chamber.

Table 2.1. Measurements of plasma parameters by Langmuir probe with various DC voltages and pressure

Parameters	DC Voltage (275 V to 375 V) & Pressure (0.12 mbar to 0.14 mbar)
Electron Temperature (T_e)	1 ~ 3.5 eV
Electron Density (n_e)	20 ~ 40 x 10^{14} m^{-3}
Plasma Potential (V_p)	290 V ~ 330 V
Floating Potential (V_f)	280 V ~ 320 V

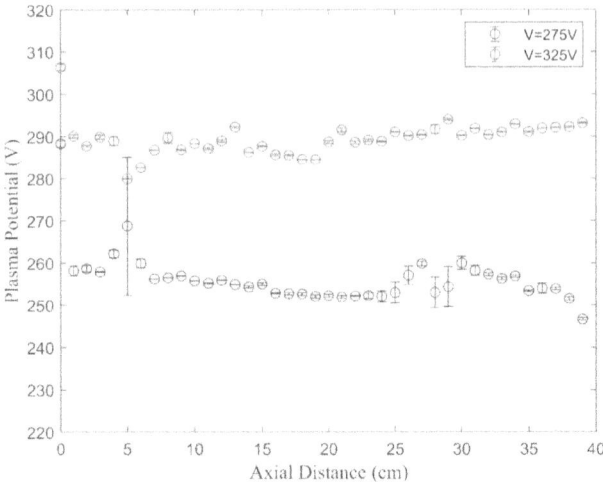

Fig. 2.12 (b). V_p at constant pressure of 0.12 mbar.

Results obtained from the Langmuir probe with varying DC voltage and vacuum pressure is shown in Table 2.1.

As illustrated in Fig. 2.9, an emissive probe with a diameter of 0.0125 mm is inserted radially into one of the upper ports of the plasma chamber. Out of the three techniques of measurement of plasma potential from emissive probe, floating potential method aptly fits in this experimental procedure. Since the values of plasma density and electron temperature in this chamber for a particular DC voltage and pressure goes well with floating point method [13, 27]. Firstly, the measurements have been taken with increase in filament current at a particular position and then observing the floating potential curve saturating at higher emission. Fig. 2.13 shows the floating potential measurements for various DC voltages and pressure. Fig. 2.13 (a) shows the floating potential for various emission at constant pressure of 0.12 mbar and DC voltage varying from 275 V to 375 V. At lower emission or filament current, floating potential remains unaffected. As soon as when emission becomes evident or increases, the V_f starts to increase till it saturates at higher emission. Principally, probe will float at plasma potential for strong emission of electrons from the probe. Hence, the measure of V_f saturating at higher emission is V_p. Similarly, the V_f is measured for various gas pressure but not much difference is observed due to not much variance of gas pressure.

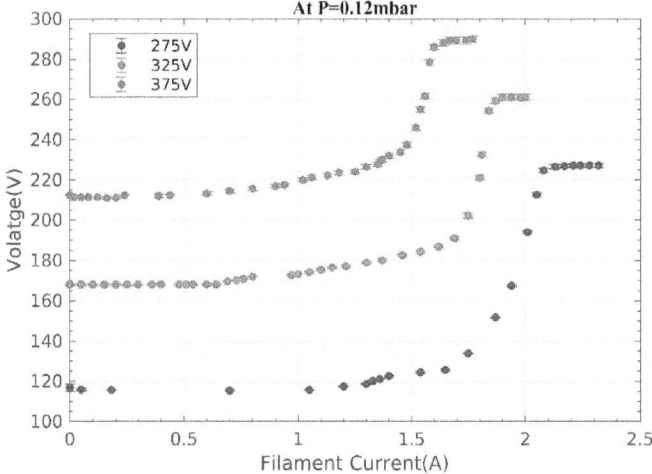

Fig. 2.13 (a) V_f at increasing filament current with varying DC voltage for constant pressure of 0.12 mbar.

After observing the probe floating at plasma potential for strong emission, the emissive probe can be moved radially in chamber and measure the plasma potential for various DC voltage and pressure. Both plasma potential and floating potential is low near the cathode due to the cathode sheath as shown in Fig. 2.14 (a). Increase of V_p and V_f at a particular position due to increase in discharge voltage is because of presence of more energetic electrons. From the Fig. 2.14 (a), it is observed that V_p and V_f increases as probe is moved away from the cathode. However, with increase in pressure both V_p and V_f decreases as shown in Fig. 2.14 (b).

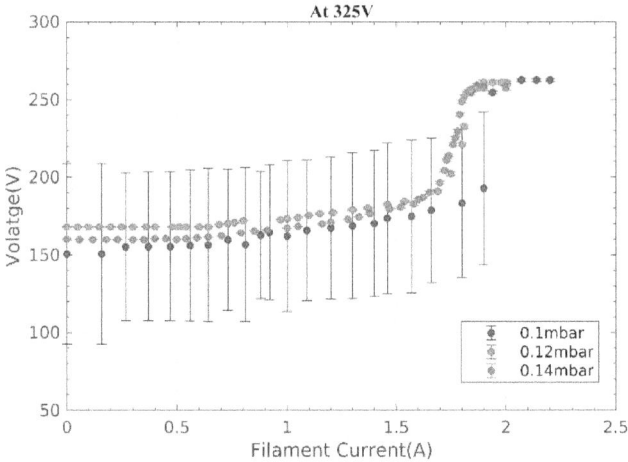

Fig. 2.13 (b) V_f for various gas pressure at constant 325 V.

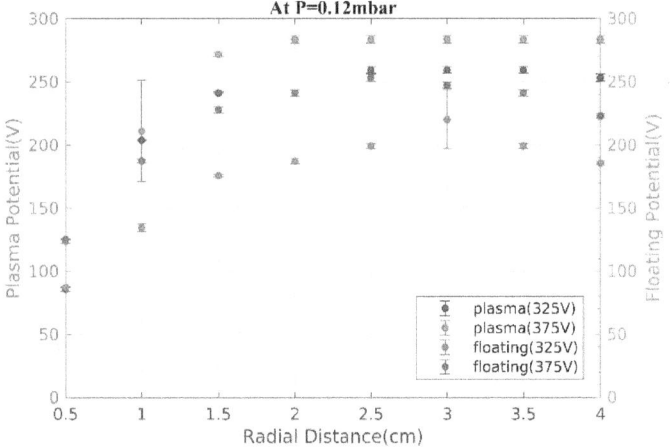

Fig. 2.14 (a) Measurement of V_p and V_f at various radial position for 325 V and 375 V discharge voltages at constant pressure 0.12 mbar. Position 1 cm corresponds to the probe near the cathode and last position to away from cathode.

As pressure increases, collision frequency of electrons increases making electron losing the energy faster. Thus, resulting in decrease of plasma and floating potential. In addition, the V_p measurement near cathode helps in estimating the electrostatic force on dust particles. Therefore, V_p and V_f has been measured for various discharge voltage and pressure. For discharge voltage of 325 V and pressure 0.12 mbar, $V_p \approx 255$ V and $V_f \approx 185$ V. For discharge voltage of 375 V and pressure 0.12 mbar, $V_p \approx 295$ V and $V_f \approx 225$ V. Contrarily, at constant discharge voltage of 325 V, not much difference is observed in $V_p \approx 255$ V and $V_f \approx 180$ V with increasing pressure.

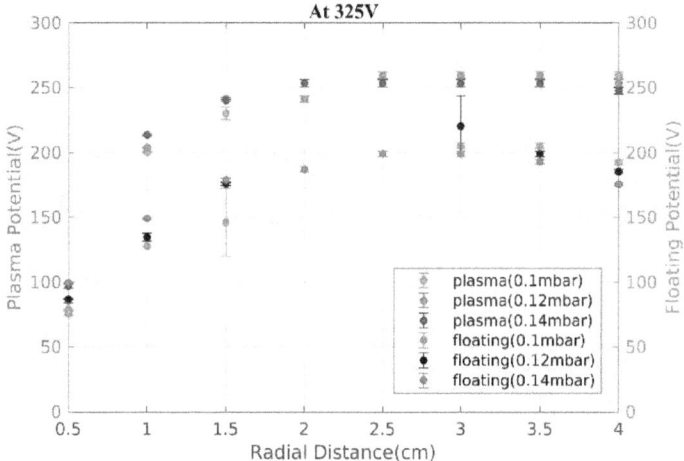

Fig. 2.14 (b) V_p and V_f with increasing pressure at constant discharge voltage of 325 V.

Accurate measurement of electron temperature (T_e) can be done by using another probe called double Langmuir probe.

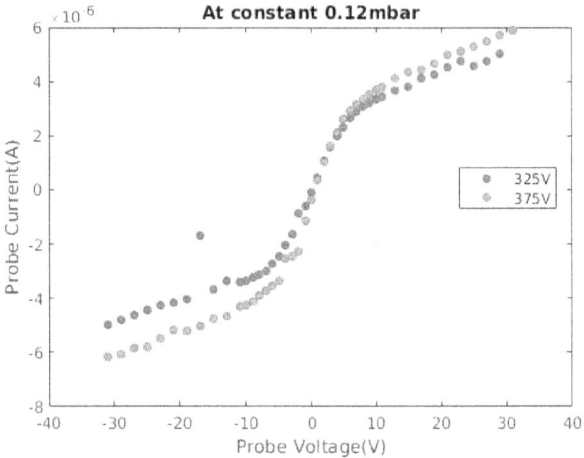

Fig. 2.15. (a) I-V curve of double Langmuir probe at constant pressure 0.12 mbar and at discharge voltages of 325 V and 375 V.

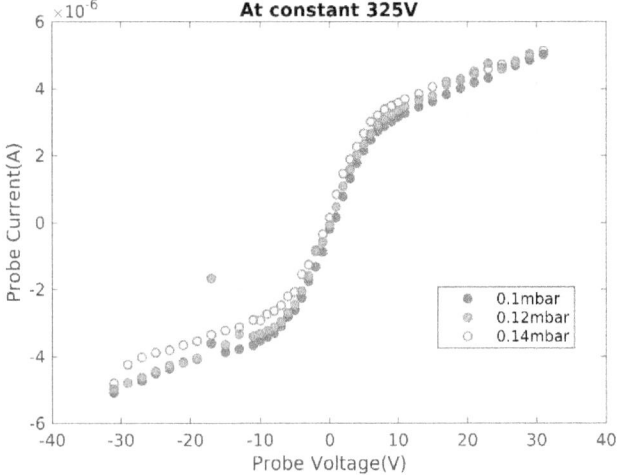

Fig. 2.15 (b) I-V Curve of double Langmuir probe at constant discharge voltage of 325 V with varying pressure.

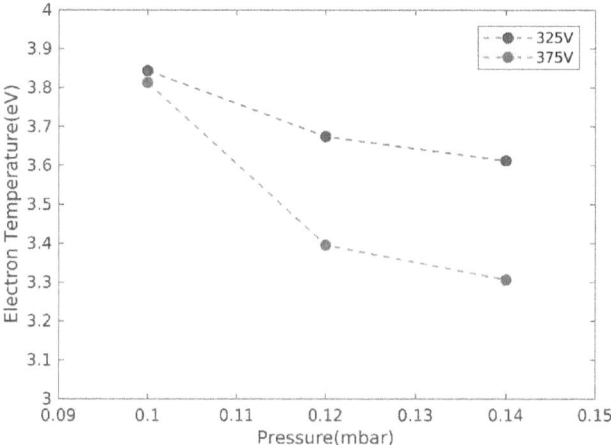

Fig. 2.16. Measurement of T_e for various discharge voltage and pressure.

Double Langmuir probe is much better than single Langmuir probe since it does not draw large currents as single probe. Fig. 2.15 displays the I-V curve of a double Langmuir probe, and T_e may be calculated using the slope of the curve drawn in the center as demonstrated in the preceding section. From the Fig. 2.16, T_e decreases for both increase in discharge voltage and pressure. As discharge voltage increases, rate of collisions increases and mean free path of the particle decreases, thus T_e decreases. Similarly with increase in pressure, number of atoms increases and hence collisionality of neutral atoms.

2.5 CONCLUSION

Probe diagnostics has been one of the best and relatively easy way to measure the plasma parameters of laboratory plasma systems. One of the great advantages of probe diagnostics is easy to use and simple electronic circuits. Further, probes can be measured spatially and temporal dimension. The tabletop setup of DPEx-II is designed such a way to study the characteristics behavior of dust particles with asymmetrical design of electrodes in DC plasma. Dust crystals, voids, dust particles in a potential well etc. are the experiments to be done in coming future. Three basic probe diagnostic techniques i.e., Langmuir probe, double Langmuir probe and Emissive probe are used in measurement of plasma parameters of DPEx-II. A detailed theory of all techniques is explained in earlier sections. The need to find plasma potential with various discharge parameters of DPEx-II will help in studies of dust particles and its levitation in vacuum chamber. Langmuir probe is a single metallic wire inserted into the plasma chamber and I-V curve is plotted with the bias voltage through oscilloscope. Plasma parameters such as plasma potential, floating potential, electron temperature, plasma density etc. are determined from the Langmuir probe with the help of MATLAB. Table 2.1 gives the detailed values of parameters measured. However, most of the measured parameters are estimated values from OML theory, and due to large fluctuations, errors in values are also large. Large fluctuations have been observed in plasma system due to ionization instability from asymmetric electrodes. Secondly, probe requires continuous cleaning due to the sputtering of ions on the probe. Hence, to overcome all these difficulties and measure the plasma potential accurately, emissive probe is introduced. As seen from the last section, plasma potential is measured more accurately in emissive probe than Langmuir probe. Direct measurement of electron temperature can be achieved from the double Langmuir probe.

Three probe techniques employed in DPEx-II instrument for measurement of plasma parameters is successfully done. In summary, it is probably to say that probe diagnostics are simple to use and have simple circuits design. Considering the huge fluctuations due to ionization instability, there is not much complexity in the measurement of parameters by probe through spatial and temporal dimension of the plasma system. However, any external electric field or foreign material introduced in plasma creates or initiate instabilities. Probe theory is also good, but it does not take account of the dynamics of changing the probe area i.e., radius of the probe which changes due to the ion sputtering on probe. There is certain necessity in improving the probe theory. Additionally, insulation of probe from ceramic should not be large due to the plasma creeping into the probe space and extending its length. Probes are difficult to use in large densities, such as in Tokamaks, Stellarators etc., due to large fluctuations or oscillations and waves. Still, probe diagnostics is the first basic and rudimental for measurement of plasma parameters. Since 1929, these techniques have been refined over a time, certainly with probe theory and as a matter of fact it's still a challenging due to the complexity of theory.

REFERENCES

1. Jaiswal, S., Bandyopadhyay, P., & Sen, A. (2015). Dusty plasma Experimental (DPEx) device for complex plasma experiments with flow. *Review of Scientific Instruments, 86*(11), 113503.
2. Jaiswal, S., Bandyopadhyay, P., & Sen, A. (2016). Experimental observation of precursor solitons in a flowing complex plasma. *Physical Review E, 93*(4), 041201.
3. Jaiswal, S., Bandyopadhyay, P., & Sen, A. (2016). Experimental investigation of flow induced dust acoustic shock waves in a complex plasma. *Physics of Plasmas, 23*(8), 083701.
4. Hariprasad, M. G., Bandyopadhyay, P., Arora, G., & Sen, A. (2018). Experimental observation of a dusty plasma crystal in the cathode sheath of a d.c. glow discharge plasma. *Physics of Plasmas, 25*(12), 123704.
5. Jaiswal, S., Bandyopadhyay, P., & Sen, A. (2016). Flowing dusty plasma experiments: Generation of flow and measurement techniques. *Plasma Sources Science and Technology, 25*(6), 065021.
6. Lieberman, M. A., & Lichtenberg, A. J. (1994). Principles of plasma discharges and materials processing. *MRS Bulletin, 30*(12), 899-901.
7. Hariprasad, M. G., Bandyopadhyay, P., Garima, A., & Sen, A. (2018). Experimental observation of a dusty plasma crystal in the cathode sheath of a d.c. glow discharge plasma. *Physics of Plasmas, 25*(12), 123704(1)-123704(7).

8. Hobbs, G. D., & Wesson, J. A. (1967). Heat flow through a langmuir sheath in the presence of electron emission. *Plasma Physics, 9*(1), 85–87.
9. Raitses, Y., Staack, D., Smirnov, A., & Fisch, N. J. (2005). Space charge saturated sheath regime and electron temperature saturation in hall thrusters. *Physics of Plasmas, 12*(7), paper 073507.
10. Matsubara, A., Sugimoto, T., Shibuya, T., Kawamura, K., Sudo, S., & Sato, K. (2003). Emissive probe measurement of electron temperature in recombining plasma produced in the linear divertor simulator TPDII. *Journal of Nuclear Materials, 313*(March), 720–724.
11. Balan, P., Schrittwieser, R., Ioniţă, C., Cabral, J. A., Figueiredo, H. F. C., Fernandes, H., Varandas, C., Adámek, J., Hron, M., Stöckel, J., Martines, E., Tichý, M., & Van Oost, G. (2003). Emissive probe measurements of plasma potential fluctuations in the edge plasma regions of tokamaks. *Review of Scientific Instruments, 74*(3), 1583–1587.
12. Ioniţă, C., Balan, P., Schrittwieser, R., Figueiredo, H. F. C., Silva, C., Varandas, C. A. F., & Galvão, R. M. O. (2004). Arrangement of emissive and cold probes for fluctuation and Reynolds Stress measurements. *Review of Scientific Instruments, 75*(10), 4331–4333.
13. Sheehan, J. P., & Hershkowitz, N. (2011). Emissive probes. *Plasma Sources Science and Technology, 20*(6), paper 063001.
14. Langmuir, I., & Compton, K. T. (1931). Electrical discharges in gases part II. Fundamental phenomena in electrical discharges. *Reviews of Modern Physics, 3*(2), 191–257.
15. Kemp, R. F., & Sellen, J. M. (1966). Plasma potential measurements by electron emissive probes. *Review of Scientific Instruments, 37*(4), 455–461.
16. Langmuir, I. (1923). The pressure effect and other phenomena in gaseous discharges. *Journal of the Franklin Institute, 196*(6), 751–762.
17. Hershkowitz, N. (1989). *'How Langmuir Probes Work,' plasma diagnostics* O. Auciello & D. L. Flamm (Eds.), 1 (pp. 113–183). Academic Press.

18. Mott-Smith, H. M., & Langmuir, I. (1926). The theory of collectors in gaseous discharges. *Physical Review, 28*(4), 727–763.
19. Smith, J. R., Hershkowitz, N., & Coakley, P. (1979). Inflection-point method of interpreting emissive probe characteristics. *Review of Scientific Instruments, 50*(2), 210.
20. Ibach, H., & Lüth, H. (2009). *Solid-state physics: An introduction to principles of materials science* (4th ed) p. 154. Springer Verlag.
21. Takamura, & S. H. U. I. C. H. I., N. (2004). Ohno, M. Y. Ye, and T. Kuwabara. "Space-Charge Limited Current from Plasma-Facing Material Surface." *Contributions to Plasma Physics, 44*(1–3), 126–137.
22. Rozhansky, V. A., & Tsendin, L. D. (2001), Chap. 3. *Transport phenomena in partially ionized plasma* (pp. 88–90). Taylor & Francis.
23. Ye, M. Y., & Takamura, S. (2000). Effect of space-charge limited emission on measurements of plasma potential using emissive probes. *Physics of Plasmas, 7*(8), 3457–3463.
24. Chen, F. F. (1965) Chap. IV. In R. H. Huddlestone & S. L. Leonard (Eds.). *Plasma diagnostic techniques p.* 184. Academic Press.
25. Hoffmann, C. R., & Lees, D. J. (1971). A differential method of measuring plasma potential. *Plasma Physics, 13*(8), 689–691.
26. Kemp, R. F., & Sellen, J. M. (1966) Plasma Potential Measurements by Electron Emissive Probes. *Review of Scientific Instruments, 37*(4), 455–461.
27. Sheehan, J. P., Raitses, Y., Hershkowitz, N., Kaganovich, I., & Fisch, N. J. (2011). A comparison of emissive probe techniques for electric potential measurements in a complex plasma. *Physics of Plasmas, 18*(7), 073501.
28. Johnson, E. O., & Malter, L. (1950). A floating double probe method for measurements in gas discharges. *Physical Review, 80*(1), 58–68.
29. Arumugam, S., Bandyopadhyay, Pintu, Singh, S., Hariprasad, M. G., Rathod, D., Arora, G., & Sen, A. (2021). DPEx-II: A new dusty plasma

device capable of producing large sized DC coulomb crystals. *Plasma Sources Science and Technology, 30*(8), 085003.

CHAPTER 3

VIRTUAL CATHODE IN PRESENCE OF DUST PARTICLES NEAR EMISSIVE WALL/ELECTRODE

3.1. INRODUCTION

When plasma is subjected to the introduction of any foreign substance, the electrons and ions in the plasma will seek to shield it. This allows the plasma to maintain its state of equilibrium. When a negatively or positively biased electrode/wall is exposed to plasma, a cloud of ions or electrons forms near the surface. This cloud is called an ion sheath or an electron sheath, respectively. The creation of such sheaths near walls or emissive surfaces has been studied and debated extensively [1-6]. The importance of the potential structure or profile in the plasma sheath depends on a number of factors, and Tongs and Langmuir were the ones who originally suggested studying it [7-8]. During last decade, it has been extensively studied using by both fluid [9-10], and kinetic model [11-12]. Classical model of one-dimensional sheath shows that plasma potential ($\phi(x)$) gradually decreases from its edge to non-emitting surface [13]. However, supplementary flow of electrons from the metallic wall, changes the potential profile substantially and it is depending on the charge density near to the wall [5]. The sheath formation in front of emissive electrode or wall is much of interest and plasma particles (electrons & ions) reaching the surface is given by Bohm sheath criterion. Riemann (1991) in his research article beautifully explains the concept of Bohm sheath criteria and pre-sheath phenomena [2]. Emissivity of the wall/electrode introduces more electrons to flow and hence modifies the sheath structure completely. Emitted electrons from wall are regarded as thermal or secondary emission. The secondary electron emission is initiated when free electrons hit a wall/electrode has been ignored because thermally emitted electrons are more useful [14]. Thermally emitted electrons current density can be found out from Richardson formula. Re-arrangement of electrons near the wall with respect to wall temperature is a self-consistent process and introduces a minimum potential region, which is typically considered as '*Virtual Cathode*' [14]. A drop in potential or a negative potential close to the wall indicates the presence of a virtual cathode, and the potential continues to rise in a consistent fashion until it approaches to the bulk plasma potential. A typical model of sheath potential in presence of virtual cathode is shown in Fig. 3.1. The physics behind the formation of virtual cathode is explained by the accumulation of space charge in front of wall/electrode due to emission of electrons from it [1]. Flow of electrons from the wall and virtual cathode are controlled by two parameters namely: wall temperature (T_w) and dust density (n_d).

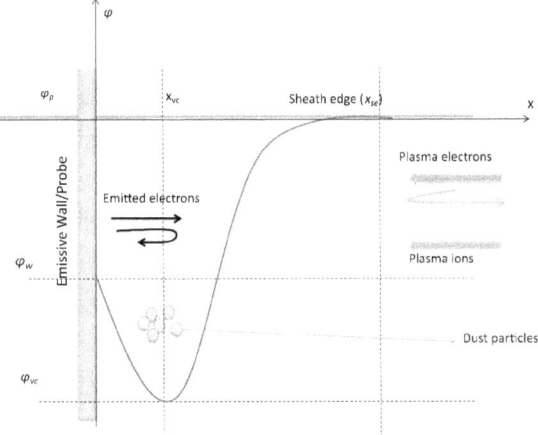

Fig. 3.1. Schematic diagram of potential profile in plasma sheath with emissive wall in a typical plasma system.

Dust particles in plasma has become one of the mainstream types of research in plasma physics due to its wide applications in variety of fields. These dust particles become charged, depending upon the actual plasma environment. Dusty plasma near to the wall/electrode or inside the sheath is of much interest since it modifies the stability of plasma sheath and Bohm condition depending on actual conditions [15-19]. This chapter describes the behavior of the virtual cathode potential close to the emissive wall/electrode in the presence of charged dust grains in the sheath to gain a better understanding of the whole phenomenon. To avoid mathematical complications in model equations, shape and size of the dust grains have been disregarded. A fluid mathematical model has been considered to get potential profile in plasma sheath, which is influenced by the wall temperature in presence of charged dust particles. Collision of ions and further ionization near to wall/electrode are considered as negligible. A brief discussion regarding Bohm criteria for ion acoustic velocity and plasma potential in the presence of charged dust grains is presented. Although, there has not been much difference for Bohm condition in dusty plasma, since most of the features associated with charged dust grains have been same for $Z_d = 1$ and $Z_d = 1000$, where Z_d is number of charges accumulated on dust grains. Ion losses to the wall/electrode are well balanced by pre-sheath, which is affectively accelerating ions towards sheath [20]. A brief review of works done on virtual cathode is described in section 2. The stationary one-dimensional fluid model to understand the virtual cathode concept is presented in section 3. Phase space diagram of the same has been plotted for differential equations, which are described in results and discussion part of section 4. Phase portrait provides a better qualitative analysis of systems because it takes a long time and a lot of work to discover analytical solutions for nonlinear dynamical system equations. Similarly, response of the potential structure as function of electron emission rate in dusty plasma has been studied with increasing electron emission rate. Variation of local plasma potential with respect to the wall/electrode temperature has been reviewed and information about double layer formation at lower dust density has been investigated close to the wall/electrode. Existence of virtual cathode is intrinsic near to the emissive wall/electrode, but on introduction of charged dust particles, potential profile is modified and behaves non-monotonously.

3.2 BRIEF REVIEW OF PREVIOUS WORK

Langmuir gave the concept of virtual cathode formation near emissive probe/wall in 1923 [21]. Child and Langmuir provided the mathematical treatment of potential profile near the emissive wall/probe and Child-Langmuir sheath [21-22]. Hobbs and Wesson were the first to offer a fluid model for understanding how electron emission affects the floating potential [3]. Theoretical study on virtual cathode and sheath structure in the presence of electron emission has been meticulously carried out [23-29]. Studies of sheath structure is very much interest in applications such as discharge plasma due to electron emission [30], thermionically emitting cathode [31], spacecraft applications [32], tokamak divertors [33, 34], meteoroids [35], moon [36], and dust particles in laboratory and space [37, 38]. In probe diagnostics, where it effects the determination of plasma characteristics (especially plasma potential), consideration of virtual cathode becomes necessary in measuring parameters [10, 39]. The released electrons usually have a distribution of energies that can be described using a temperature parameter T_w. The sheath potential is determined by the ratio of emitted electron temperature to plasma temperature, according to Sheehan *et al.* [13, 40]. The model says that as the temperature ratio gets closer to one, the sheath potential should also get closer to zero. This prediction was confirmed by the results of PIC simulations [39] and observations [41] of the sheath around a thermionically generating cathode in the afterglow of an RF plasma. This work also included a generalization of the Bohm criterion to account for secondary electron emission (see equation (5) of [39]). Campanell *et al.,* [42] using one-dimensional PIC simulations studied barriers with a secondary electron emission coefficient greater than unity. To put it another way, there were no sheaths if the emission coefficient was close to unity, and there were "inverse sheaths" when the secondary electron emission coefficient was much higher than unity [42].

3.3. MATHEMATICAL MODEL

A schematic diagram of behavior of potential is drawn vaguely to study the characteristic of virtual cathode and non-monotonic behavior of potential profile inside the plasma sheath as shown in Fig. 3.1. Virtual cathode is formed near to wall at distance $x = x_{vc}$ and corresponding potential is given as $\varphi = \varphi_{vc}$. Variation of local plasma potential $\varphi(x)$ is from $x = 0$ to $x = x_{se}$ (se: sheath edge). In equilibrium, floating potential of wall becomes equal to plasma potential at x_{se}, at which sheath edge potential is equal to bulk plasma potential. Floating potential is relatively easier to find at weekly electron emission since potential is independent of T_w. However, for strong electron emission, it fluctuates with increasing T_w [14]. When a metal is heated to a temperature by applying current through it, thermally agitated electron is emitted from the surface. This thermionic temperature dependent emitted electrons flow into the plasma sheath and creates an instability. Hence, the potential profile inside the sheath also changes. The change of potential structures has been observed in recent studies with respect to thermionic electron emission and secondary electron emission [43-46]. The thermionic current density (j_{rd}) can be estimated by Richardson-Dushmann classical expression, which is stated as,

$$j_{rd} = AT_w^2 exp\left(\frac{-W_f}{k_B T_w}\right) \qquad (3.1)$$

where, W_f is the work function of material and A is Richardson constant which depends on property of metal and k_B -Boltzmann's constant. In addition, average emitted electron velocity (v_w) can be written as

$$v_w \cong \sqrt{\frac{2k_B T_w}{\pi m_e}} \qquad (3.2)$$

where, m_e is mass of electron. A constructive result has been obtained with this thermionic emission law throughout this mathematical model. Electrons sticking on the dust particles are considered here, whereas other process of reflection/transmission has been neglected. The electric field at the sheath edge is negligible since electron density is less [3]. Density of thermionic emitted electrons ($n_{ee}(x)$) is considered as constant within the sheath and thermal equilibrium with the wall/electrode. Boltzmann relation for emitted electrons is given as

$$n_{ee}(x) = n_{ee}^0 \exp\left[\frac{-e(\varphi_w - \varphi(x))}{k_B T_w}\right] \quad (3.3)$$

where, φ_w is wall potential, e is the charge of electron and

$$n_{ee}^0 = j_{rd}/e\, v_w \quad (3.4)$$

Here, density of plasma electrons (n_{pe}) is assumed Maxwellian and described by Boltzmann relation. Whereas ions, which are heavier than electrons have same energy at any place and mostly referred as cold ions such as that density of ions n_i and n_e are given as

$$n_i(x) = n_{i,se}\left[1 + \frac{2e(\varphi_{se} - \varphi(x))}{m_i v_0^2}\right]^{-\frac{1}{2}} \quad (3.5)$$

$$n_{pe}(x) = n_{pe,se} \exp\left[\frac{-e(\varphi_{se} - \varphi(x))}{k_B T_{pe}}\right] \quad (3.6)$$

where, T_{pe} is plasma electron temperature, φ_{se} is sheath edge potential at x_{se}, m_i is the mass of ions, v_0 is ion thermal velocity and $\varphi(x)$ is a potential variation from sheath edge to wall, respectively. $n_{pe,se}$ and $n_{i,se}$ are density of plasma electrons and ions at the sheath edge. Near the beginning of the sheath area, a breakdown of quasi-neutrality can be seen [4]. According to assumption, the dust particle number density is the same in the sheath and equilibrium plasma i.e., $Z_d n_{d0} = Z_d n_d$, for linear case [15]. The plasma is considered one-dimensional sheath and in thermal equilibrium, such as that potential in plasma sheath is given by Poisson's equation for $x > 0$ as

$$\frac{d^2\varphi(x)}{dx^2} = \frac{-e}{\varepsilon_0}[n_i(x) - n_e(x) - n_{rd} - Z_d n_d(\varphi(x))] \qquad (3.7)$$

where, $n_d(\varphi(x))$ is the dust density which is assumed to be dependent on $\varphi(x)$ and also another condition where independent of $\varphi(x)$ and n_{rd} is density of thermionic emitted electrons near to the wall at the minimum potential φ_{vc} can be written as

$$n_{ee}(x) = n_{ee}^0 \exp\left[\frac{-e(\varphi_w - \varphi_{vc})}{k_B T_w}\right] \equiv n_{rd} \qquad (3.8)$$

Quasi-neutrality condition for plasma at the sheath edge (x_{se}) is given as

$$n_{pe,se} + n_{rd} + Z_{d0} n_{d0} = n_{i,se} = n_0 \qquad (3.9)$$

n_0 is density of distant equilibrium plasma which is approximately equals to $n_{i,se}$. Making above Eqn. (3.7) to dimensionless form i.e. normalizing velocity, potential, emitted electrons and dust density as follows,

$$\phi = \frac{e(\varphi_{se} - \varphi)}{k_B T_{pe}}, M = \frac{v_0}{C_{is}}, \alpha = \frac{n_{rd}}{n_0}, \beta = \frac{Z_d n_d}{n_0} \qquad (3.10)$$

where, $C_{is} = \sqrt{k_B T_{pe}/m_i}$ is ion sound velocity and M is normalized ionic velocity or Mach velocity, which is necessity condition for Bohm criterion, and T_{pe} is plasma electron temperature. Hence, electron and ion density can be written as

$$n_i(x) = n_0\left[1 + \frac{2\phi}{M^2}\right]^{\frac{-1}{2}} \qquad (3.11)$$

$$n_{pe}(x) = (n_0 - n_{rd} - Z_d n_d)\exp(-\phi) \qquad (3.12)$$

Substituting Eqn. (3.10), (3.11) and (3.12) in Eqn. (3.7) and taking electric field as $E = -d\varphi/dx$, then given differential equation is solved by first integral,

$$\frac{1}{2}\varepsilon^2 = M^2\left(\sqrt{1 + \frac{2\phi}{M^2}} - 1\right) + (1 - \alpha - \beta)(e^{-\phi} - 1) - \alpha\phi - \beta\phi \qquad (3.13)$$

where, ε is dimensionless electric field which is given by

$$\varepsilon = E\sqrt{\frac{\varepsilon_0}{n_0 k_B T_{pe}}} \qquad (3.14)$$

Solution of Eqn. (3.13) is lengthy and tedious, hence stability analysis of the same as been employed to get an idea of the equilibrium solutions or points. The right hand side of the Eqn. (3.13) is made to zero for small values of ϕ ($\ll 1$), which gives useful information about the behavior of ϕ. Eqn. (3.13) can be written as

$$\frac{1}{2}\left(\frac{d\phi}{d\eta}\right)^2 + V(\phi) = 0 \qquad (3.15)$$

where, $V(\phi)$ is given as

$$V(\phi) = -M^2\left(\sqrt{1 + \frac{2\phi}{M^2}} - 1\right) - (1 - \alpha - \beta)\left(e^{-\phi} - 1\right) + \alpha\phi + \beta\phi \qquad (3.16)$$

The phase portrait of above equation with varying α, is shown in Fig. 2. It is clear from Fig. 3.2 that as α increases, the stability of the system moves towards the irregularity, irrespective of Z_d and n_d value. The curve which has two stable points i.e., at origin and farther away from origin for $\alpha = 0.2$, moves away from stability for $\alpha = 0.6$, as two points becomes closer and destroys itself at origin as α increases. This shows that dependence of potential $\phi(x)$ on α is strong. Dependence of α ($\alpha < 1$) on T_w and ϕ_{vc} can be written as from Eqn. (3.10)

$$\alpha = \frac{n_{ee}^0}{n_0} exp\left[\frac{T_{pe}}{T_w}(\phi_w - \phi_{vc})\right] \qquad (3.17)$$

Bohm's criterion is governed to sheath edge i.e., at asymptotic limit $\lambda_D/L \to 0$ and is a mandatory condition for strong fields to decay at λ_D. This condition insists ions to have at least ion acoustic velocity (Bohm velocity) to enter the sheath region [4].

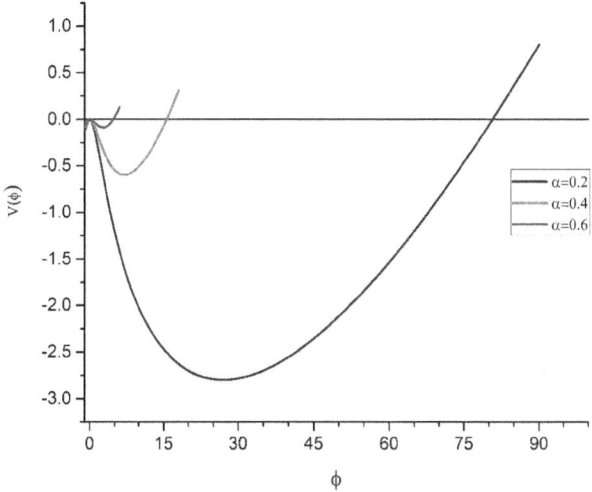

Fig. 3.2: Phase portrait space diagram of a normalized potential ϕ

The right-hand side of Eqn. (3.13) can be expanded in terms of Taylor's series and applying above condition, such that Bohm criterion is established for dusty plasma as

$$M^2 \geq \frac{1}{1-\alpha-\beta} + N^2 \qquad (3.18)$$

where, N^2 is a dimensionless velocity [14]. This equation clearly indicates that if there is non-emissive wall and no dusty plasma, then the equation retains its originality condition [47]

$$M^2 \geq 1 \qquad (3.19)$$

Conditionality of formation of virtual cathode is given by threshold wall temperature ($T_{w,th}$), such as that the potential difference ($\varphi_{vc} - \varphi_w$) changes its sign as wall temperature increases [14] i.e., $\varphi_{vc} < \varphi_w$ for $T_w > T_{w,th}$. The potential difference is proportional to dust density, which is dependent on dust potential. This is considered as non-linear behavior such that, the equation becomes

$$\varphi_{vc} - \varphi_w \propto n_d(\phi_d) \qquad (3.20)$$

The potential difference (φ_{vc}- φ_w) can be numerically solved from Eqn. (3.8) to (3.10), and plotting with respect to T_w, gives an idea of potential behavior in presence of charged dust grains and virtual cathode. β is normalized dust density variable, which acts an important aspect in formation of virtual cathode as discussed in later section. If potential difference is taken in linear form, and n_d is kept as constant variable, independent of dust potential (ϕ_d) in (φ_{vc}- φ_w) equation, then equation can be derived as

$$(\varphi_{vc} - \varphi_w) = \frac{k_B T_w}{e} \ln\left(\frac{Z_d n_d \alpha}{n_{ee}^0 \beta}\right) \quad (3.21)$$

3.4. NUMERICAL RESULTS AND DISCUSSION

An effort has been made for realistic approach by making use of experimental plasma properties. Taking into consideration an Argon plasma with a density of approximately $10^7 \sim 10^{11}$ cm^{-3} and a plasma electron temperature of T_{pe} = (0.2 ~ 1.2) eV [48]. Unperturbed density of ions (n_i) and electrons (n_e) are assumed to be equal. The potential profile of plasma is measured between $x_w < x < x_{vc}$. ϕ_{vc} and α can be evaluated from Eqn. (3.13). Two conditions have been discussed, with $Z_d = 1$ and $Z_d = 1000$ for non-linearity case and one with linear case in front of tungsten emissive wall/electrode. For continuous thermionic electron emission, the potential to the wall/electrode is supplied by stabilized DC power. In last section, phase space was drawn to identify the nature of solutions with variables. Therefore, the Hamiltonian system of equation can be represented in phase space diagram from which relatively simpler equation is deduced as

$$\frac{\varepsilon^2}{2} + V(\phi) = f \quad (3.22)$$

where, f is characterized as a scalar function known as Hamiltonian function and orbits of the Hamiltonian dynamical system in ε-ϕ plane are the curves corresponding to constant f and $\zeta(\phi)$ is generalized potential or Sagdeev potential which is given by

$$\zeta(\phi) = -\left(\frac{1}{1-\alpha-\beta} + N^2\right)\left(\sqrt{1 + \frac{2\phi}{\left(\frac{1}{1-\alpha-\beta} + N^2\right)}} - 1\right)$$

$$-(1-\alpha-\beta)(e^{-\phi} - 1) + \alpha\phi + \beta\phi \qquad (3.23)$$

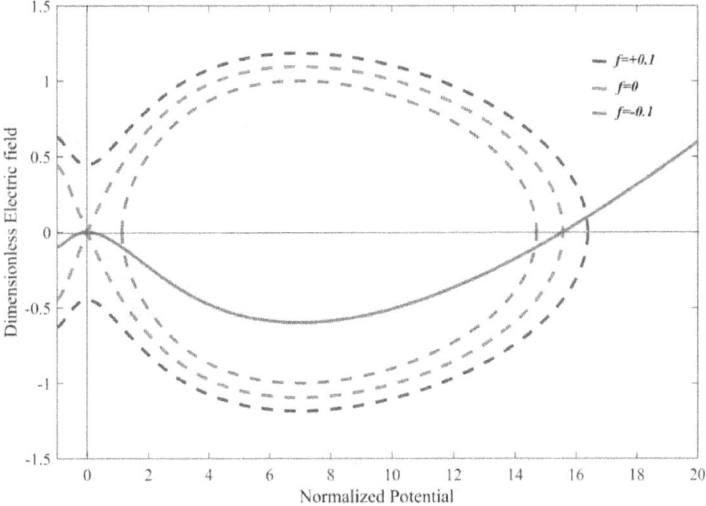

Fig. 3.3. Phase-space diagram between dimensionless electric field $\varepsilon(\phi)$ and normalized potential (ϕ) as in Eqn. (3.22). Solid line corresponds to generalized potential of Eqn. (3.23).

Throughout numerical analysis, dust density is varied from $10^1 \sim 10^6$ cm^{-3}, which is relatively lower, compared to the plasma density and emitted electrons density. For Eqn. (3.22) to be negative $f < 0$ and for $\alpha = 0.4$, Fig. 3.3 shows that $\phi(x)$ is periodic around the normalized potential, which is not possible in the presence of emissive wall. Whereas, for $f > 0$, there are two solutions i.e., for $\phi > 0$ and $\phi < 0$. For $\phi > 0$, there is one solution or root at $\varepsilon(\phi_{vc}) = 0$ and other solutions for $\phi < 0$ becomes unrealistic since potential is negative and imaginary here. For $f = 0$, we get two solutions, $\varepsilon(\phi_{vc}) = 0$ and at equilibrium point $\phi = 0$, $\varepsilon = 0$. The continuous bold line is the generalized potential profile, which is same as Fig. 3.2. Therefore, for large values of x, effective potential becomes zero i.e., approaches to plasma potential.

For $f = 0$, Fig. 3.4, describes the physical solution of potential structure near the wall for different values of α and normalizing speed $N^2=1$. Model agrees with the potential structure of Fig. 3.1 near to emissive wall. As α decreases, the potential becomes more positive and possibility of forming virtual cathode diminishes. That is the reason, at $\alpha = 0.1$ potential is very large and at $\alpha = 0.4$ is very less positive. Both the graph Fig. 3.3 and 3.4, showed no signs of change with or without inclusion of Z_d and with change in dust density.

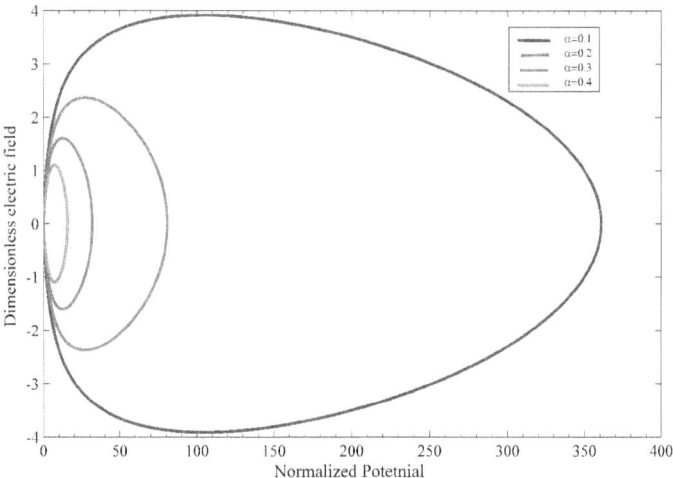

Fig. 3.4. Phase space diagram for $f = 0$ and $\alpha = n_{rd}/n_0$. This diagram shows the physical solution of potential structure formation with increase in thermionic emission.

To find the threshold temperature for which virtual cathode occurs, potential differences ($\varphi_{vc} - \varphi_w$) as a function of wall temperature has been plotted considering $Z_d = 1$ and shown in Fig. 3.5.

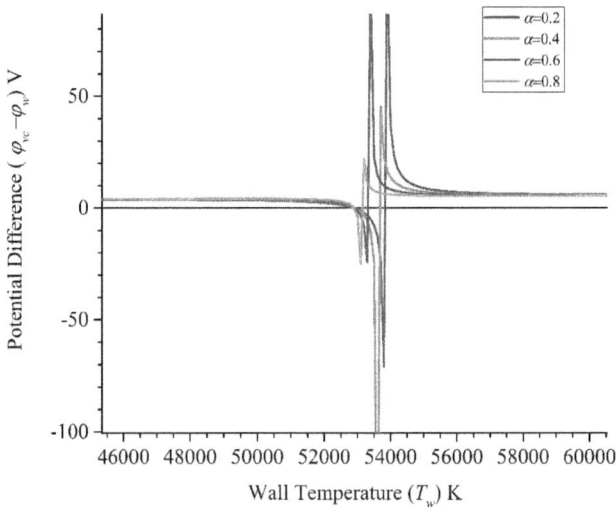

Fig. 3.5(a)

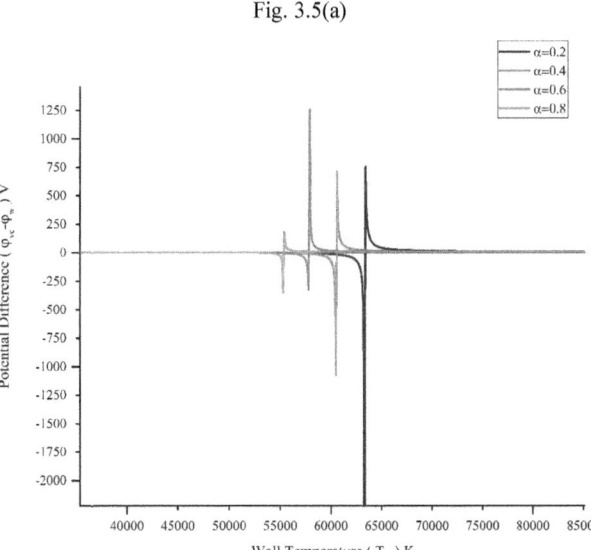

Fig. 3.5(b)

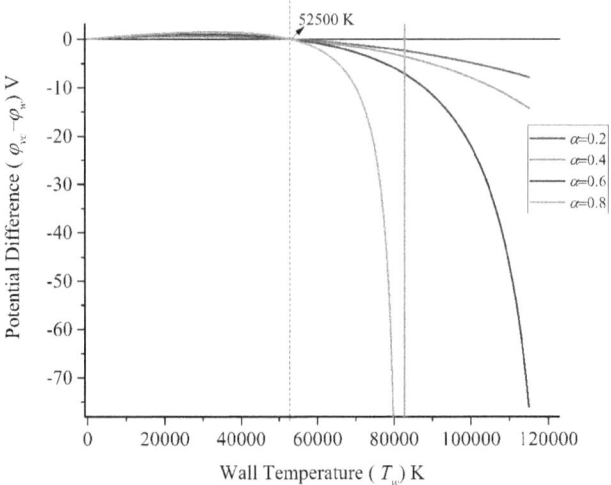

Fig. 3.5(c)

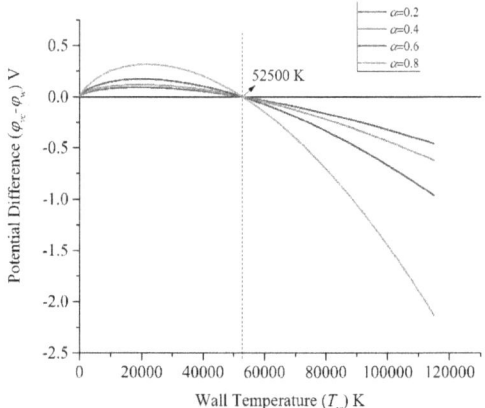

Fig. 3.5(d)

Fig. 3.5. Potential difference as a function of wall temperature for different n_{d0} and α is plotted at $Z_d = 1$. Variance of potential difference at (a) $n_{d0} = 10^3$ cm^{-3} (b) $n_{d0} = 10^4$ cm^{-3} (c) $n_{d0} = 10^5$ cm^{-3} (d) $n_{d0} = 10^6$ cm^{-3}

Now, considering with dust grain charge $Z_d = 1000$, and plotting in the Fig. 3.6 as shown below.

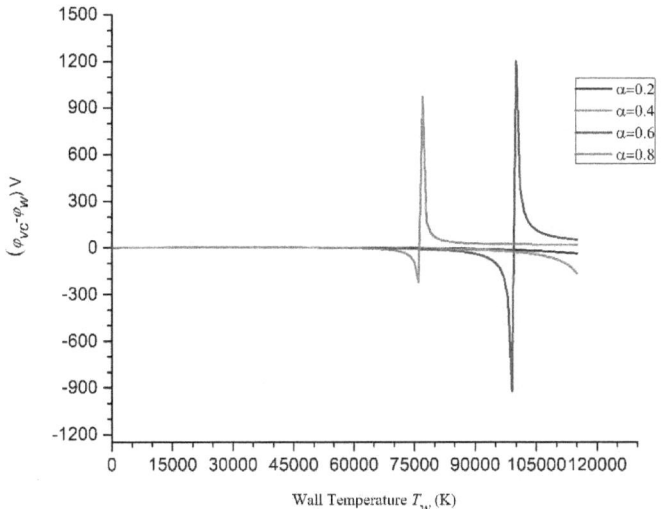

Fig. 3.6 (a)

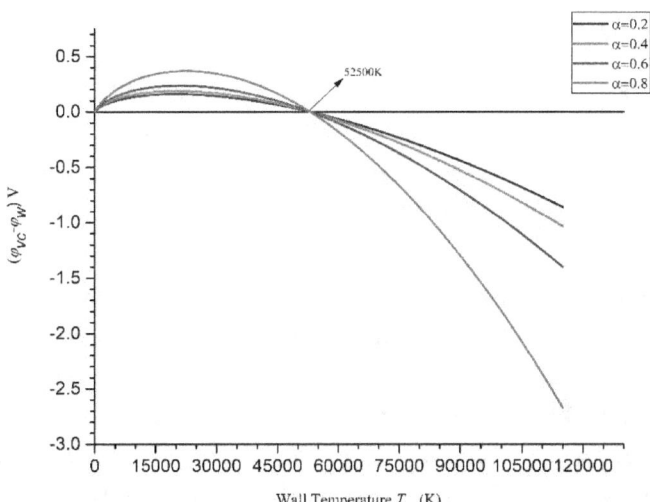

Fig. 3.6 (b)

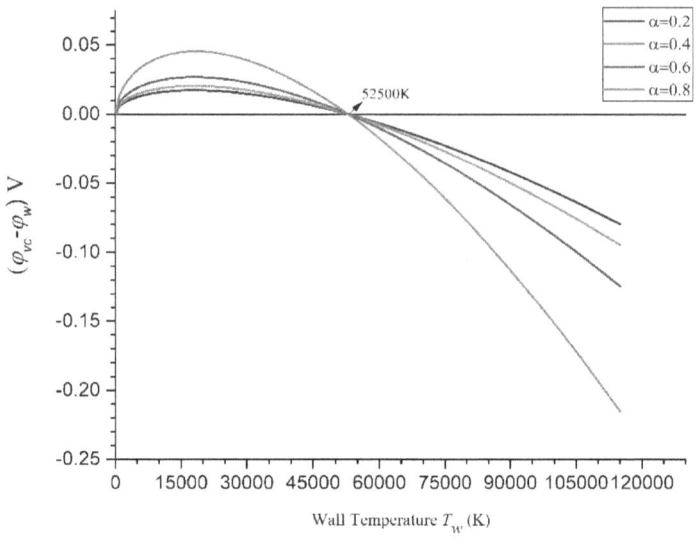

Fig. 3.6(C)

Fig. 3.6. Potential difference as a function of wall temperature for different dust density and α is plotted for Z_d = 1000. Variance of potential difference at (a) n_{d0} =10^1 cm^{-3} (b) n_{d0} =10^2 cm^{-3} (c) n_{d0} =10^3 cm^{-3}

3.4 (a) For Z_d = 1:

Virtual cathode is developed at threshold wall temperature $T_{w,th}$ when the condition $\varphi_{vc} - \varphi_w < 0$ is satisfied. Fig. 3.5(a) for n_{d0} =10^3 cm^{-3} with increase in α from 0.2 to 0.8, the potential difference value ($\varphi_{vc} - \varphi_w$) shows a sudden surge of peaks at almost same value of T_w. This shows that there is a high potential drop inside the sheath region, which is accountable to formation of positive ions sheath around negatively charged dust grains. Hence, generation of sheath with high potential drops in presence of charged dust particles becomes prominent and two space charge layers is developed, which is termed as double layer. This is where the screening of dust becomes important, where ϕ_d plays the key role in forming double layer. From α = 0.2 to 0.6, potential difference has large values recognizing two space charge layers holding high potential drops. At α = 0.8, strong emission reduces the positively charged sheath, hence reducing potential drop. In Fig. 3.5(b), for $n_{d0} = 10^4$ cm^{-3} as α increases, double layer forms at relatively less value of T_w. In this case, the increase of n_{d0} makes φ_{vc} to become more positive at the same value of α. Also, the potential drop decreases as α increases such that φ_{vc} starts decreasing. It is also clear that for higher α, the double layer formation takes place even at lower value of T_w. But at $n_{d0} = 10^5$ cm^{-3}, it is observed that for weakly emission of electrons, potential difference value shows a change in sign at $T_w = 52500$ °K and termed as threshold wall temperature $(T_{w,th})$. Thus, Fig. 3.5 (c) shows the existence of virtual cathode in dusty plasma at weakly emission regime, which shows as a linear behavior where n_{d0} is increased and collection of charges is less by dust grains. Interestingly this threshold temperature remains same with increasing α (up to 0.6). Therefore, at weakly emission condition, there is no double layer formation as lack of electrons to shield dust particles. However, at higher emission ($\alpha > 0.6$), formation of double layer is noticed. Fig. 3.5(d) shows the appearance of virtual cathode for all values of α at $n_{d0} = 10^6$ cm^{-3}. This density is called threshold dust density $(n_{d0,th})$. Interesting thing to note that for $n_{d0} \geq 10^6$ cm^{-3}, the double layer vanishes and behaves more like as linear and collective effects. This condition may be acted as a multi component or three component plasma systems with an extra negative charge due to charged dust grains. Thus, there are two conditions to occur a virtual cathode near to the wall in dusty plasma: threshold wall temperature $(T_{w,th})$ and threshold dust density $(n_{d0,th})$.

3.4 (b) For Z_d=1000

The same double layer is observed when dust charge is included i.e., $Z_d = 1000$ as shown in Fig. 3.6(a). In this condition, virtual cathode forms at very smaller density n_{d0}. In Fig. 3.6(b), where $n_{d0} = 10^1$ cm^{-3}, shows the potential difference changing the sign at 52500 °K wall temperature. It is also observed in Fig. 3.6(c), with increasing n_{d0}, and in this condition, the potential difference becomes more and more negative. Hence, it confirms that the consideration of dust charge value enhanced the formation of virtual cathode at very smaller n_{d0}.

If a voltage is applied to emissive electrode/wall, then there is a material dependence threshold temperature (depends on work function of material) due to which the instability initiates in plasma. Hence, studies of virtual cathode and its associated instability as a function of wall materials are particularly important, and also it is important to know how it behaves in presence of magnetic field too, which could be considered as future course of study.

3.4 (c) $n_d = n_{d0}$

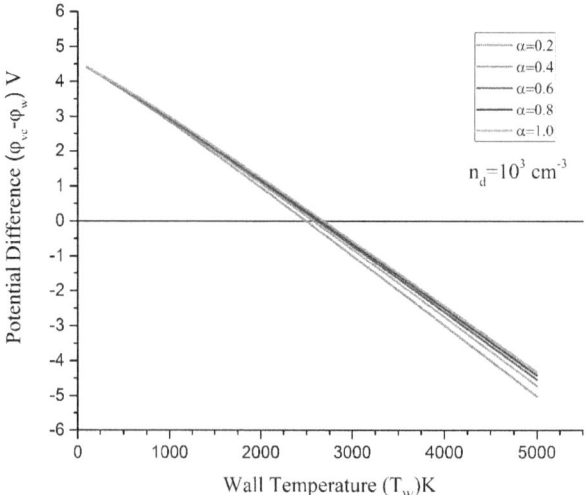

Fig. 3.7(a)

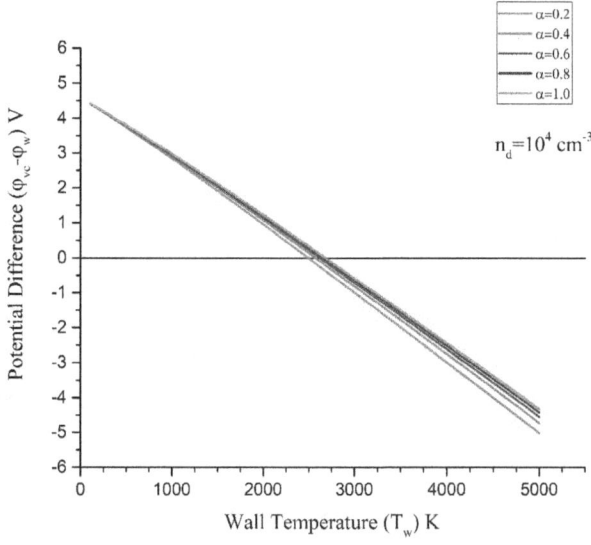

Fig. 3.7(b)

Fig. 3.7. Plot of potential difference for $n_d=n_{d0}$ at various α. For $\alpha = 0.2$, $T_{w,th}=$ 2494 °K; $\alpha = 0.4$, $T_{w,th} = 2573$ °K; $\alpha = 0.6$, $T_{w,th} = 2621$ °K; $\alpha = 0.8$, $T_{w,th} = 2656$ °K; $\alpha = 1.0$, $T_{w,th} = 2685$ °K are respective values for irrespective of n_d.

Dust density (n_d) is considered here as independent of dust potential (ϕ_d). n_d is varied from 10^3 to 10^6 cm^{-3} and Z_d from 1 to 1000. Fig. shows that, $T_{w,th}$ values varies from 2494 °K to 2685 °K as α increases from 0.1 to 1. Without dust grains near the wall, $T_{w,th}$ was around 1750 °K [14]. Because of introduction of dust grains and its capability of gaining charges from the surrounding plasma, formation of virtual cathode is formed at higher wall potential value, hence $T_{w,th}$ at higher value. There is not much impact of n_d and Z_d on the varying of its value on threshold temperature for formation of virtual cathode. But as bulk plasma density (n_0) is increased, the $T_{w,th}$ moves towards the higher value. As more density is increased, accumulation of charges on dust grain increases thus delaying the formation of virtual cathode.

3.5. CONCLUSION

From qualitative and quantitative analysis of potential profiles at different T_w, number of charges on dust grains and dust grain densities, the formation of virtual cathode near to wall/electrode has been observed, in a system consisting of ions, electrons and negatively charged dust particles. It has been found that, for $n_d(\phi_d)$ virtual cathode appears at $T_w = 52500$ °K, which is also called as threshold wall temperature. Hence, the existence of virtual cathode in dusty plasma is observed at very high T_w which is very much higher than in the absence of charged dust grains [14]. Only ϕ_d and Z_d is effectively considered here for complete understanding by neglecting the shape and size of dust grain and found that the non-linearity of n_d (ϕ_d) gives at higher T_w. This high T_w can be attributed to the considered assumption of properties associated with charged dust grains. It is seen that, for $Z_d = 1$, the virtual cathode is observed at $n_{d0} = 10^6$ cm^{-3}, whereas for $Z_d = 1000$, the same is observed at very small dust density conditions i.e., $n_{d0} = 10^2$ cm^{-3}. For weekly emission region and $Z_d = 1$ at $n_d = 10^5$ cm^{-3}, virtual cathode has been observed at $T_{w,th}$. Also at lower dust density, the observed potential difference is very large because electrons emitted from emissive wall has already induced a low potential ($\varphi_{vc} < \varphi_w$). On the other hand, as dust particles are introduced near to the wall, the potential difference ($\varphi_{vc} > \varphi_w$) becomes positive. To reduce φ_{vc}, or to make more negative φ_{vc}, T_w is increased so that large number of electrons can be accumulated near the wall. As n_d increases, the potential difference value ($\varphi_{vc} - \varphi_w$) decreases. The spike in Fig. 3.5(a), (b) and (c) is owing to formation of double layer. Whereas for $Z_d=1000$, the trend follows the same, i.e., double layer formation at $n_d = 10^1$ cm^{-3} for higher emission but at $n_d=10^2$ cm^{-3} virtual cathode is observed. Increasing dust density, the potential becomes lesser and more negative, and behaves linearly at higher T_w.

This is the first time that appearance of double layer is observed in dusty plasma in front of emissive wall. Double layer forming at lower dust density shows that space charge layer with high potential drop and is developed in presence of charged dust particles and surface of dust particles acts as an equipotential surface. Also, calculated values clearly shows that double layer does not occur for $Z_d = 1$ at $n_{d,th} \geq 10^6$ cm^{-3} and for $Z_d = 1000$ at $n_{d,th} \geq 10^1$ cm^{-3}. Addition of dust particles in plasma sheath tends to delay the formation of virtual cathode and hence increasing the value of T_w. Whereas for linear case, there is no double layer formation and small increase of $T_{w,th}$ as compared to absence of dust grains. This is the reason where dust grains show collective behavior at low bulk density (n_0). If we increase n_0, then $T_{w,th}$ will also increase, as increase of density, the particle accumulation by dust grains increases and delaying the formation of virtual cathode. It is also confirmed that virtual cathode is formed between $T_{w,th} = 2494$ °K to 2685 °K in a dusty plasma system. It is clear from the observation that T_w effectively depends on wall material. For given dust density, there are different variations of potential profile in a sheath near to the wall for different α, n_0, and Z_d, which has been discussed in detail in this work. Properties associated with dusty plasma and its non-linearity dependence of screening potential can be considered for future study with different materials. Further, virtual cathode in magnetized plasma can be examined with different emissions.

REFERENCES

1. Intrator, T., Cho, M. H., Wang, E. Y., Hershkowitz, N., Diebold, D., & DeKock, J. (1988). The virtual cathode as a transient double sheath. *Journal of Applied Physics*, *64*(6), 2927–2933.
2. Riemann, K. U. (1991). The Bohm criterion and sheath formation. *Journal of Physics D: Applied Physics*, *24*(4), 493–518.
3. Hobbs, G. D., & Wesson, J. A. (1967). Heat flow through a Langmuir sheath in the presence of electron emission. *Plasma Physics*, *9*(1), 85–87.
4. Allen, J. E. (2009). The plasma–sheath boundary: Its history and Langmuir's definition of the sheath edge. *Plasma Sources Science and Technology*, *18*(1), 014004.

5. Franklin, R. N. (2003). The plasma–sheath boundary region. *Journal of Physics D: Applied Physics*, *36*(22), R309–R320.
6. Bittencourt, J. A. (2004). *Fundamentals of plasma physics*. Springer Science & Business Media.
7. Tonks, L., & Langmuir, I. (1929). A general theory of the plasma of an arc. *Physical Review*, *34*(6), 876–922.
8. Langmuir, I. (1929). The interaction of electron and positive ion space charges in cathode sheaths. *Physical Review*, *33*(6), 954–989.
9. Takamura, S. H. U. I. C. H. I., Ohno, N., Ye, M. Y., & Kuwabara, T. (2004). Space-Charge Limited Current from Plasma-Facing Material Surface. *Contributions to Plasma Physics, 44*(1-3), 126-137.
10. Ye, M. Y., & Takamura, S. (2000). Effect of space-charge limited emission on measurements of plasma potential using emissive probes. *Physics of Plasmas*, *7*(8), 3457–3463.
11. Yu, M. Y., Saleem, H., & Luo, H. (1992). Dusty plasma near a conducting boundary. *Physics of Fluids B: Plasma Physics*, *4*(10), 3427–3431.
12. Gyergyek, T., Jurčič-Zlobec, B., Čerček, M., & Kovačič, J. (2009). Sheath structure in front of an electron emitting electrode immersed in a two-electron temperature plasma: A fluid model and numerical solutions of the Poisson equation. *Plasma Sources Science and Technology*, *18*(3), 035001.
13. Sheehan, J. P., Hershkowitz, N., Kaganovich, I. D., Wang, H., Raitses, Y., Barnat, E. V., Weatherford, B. R., & Sydorenko, D. (2013). Kinetic theory of plasma sheaths surrounding electron-emitting surfaces. *Physical Review Letters*, *111*(7), 075002.
14. Tierno, S. P., Donoso, J. M., Domenech-Garret, J. L., & Conde, L. (2016). Existence of a virtual cathode close to a strongly electron emissive wall in low density plasmas. *Physics of Plasmas*, *23*(1), 013503.
15. Shukla, P. K. (2001). A survey of dusty plasma physics. *Physics of Plasmas*, *8*(5), 1791–1803.

16. Shukla, P. K., & Mamun, A. A. (2015). *Introduction to dusty plasma physics*. CRC Press.
17. Luo, H., & Yu, M. Y. (1997). Shielding of dust grains at the edge of an equilibrium plasma. *Physical Review E*, *56*(1), 1270–1272.
18. Benilov, M. S., & Shukla, P. K. (2000). Bohm criterion for a plasma composed of electrons and positive dust grains. *Physical Review E*, *63*(1), 016410.
19. Samarian, A. A., Vladimirov, S. V., & James, B. W. (2005, October). Experiments on alignment of dust particles in plasma sheath. In *AIP Conference Proceedings* (Vol 799. No. 1, pp 553–556). American Institute of Physics
20. Robertson, S. (2013). Sheaths in laboratory and space plasmas. *Plasma Physics and Controlled Fusion*, *55*(9), 093001.
21. Langmuir, I. (1923). The effect of space charge and initial velocities on the potential distribution and thermionic current between parallel plane electrodes. *Physical Review*, *21*(4), 419–435.
22. Child, C. D. (1911). Discharge from hot CaO. *Physical Review*, *32*(5), 492–511.
23. Guernsey, R. L., & Fu, J. H. M. (1970). Potential distribution surrounding a photo-emitting, plate in a dilute plasma. *Journal of Geophysical Research*, *75*(16), 3193–3199.
24. Li, W., Ma, J. X., Li, J.-J., Zheng, Y.b., & Tan, M.-S. (2012). Measurement of virtual cathode structures in a plasma sheath caused by secondary electrons. *Physics of Plasmas*, *19*(3), 030704.
25. Bohm, D. (1949). *The characteristics of electrical discharges in magnetic fields* A. Guthrie & R. K. Wakerling (Eds.). McGraw-Hill.
26. Hershkowitz, N. (2005). Sheaths: More complicated than you think. *Physics of Plasmas*, *12*(5), 055502.

27. Tskhakaya, D. D., Shukla, P. K., Eliasson, B., & Kuhn, S. (2005). Theory of the plasma sheath in a magnetic field parallel to the wall. *Physics of Plasmas*, *12*(10), 103503.
28. Riemann, K.-U. (1997). The influence of collisions on the plasma sheath transition. *Physics of Plasmas*, *4*(11), 4158–4166.
29. Ma, J.-X., & Yu, M. Y. (1995). Electrostatic sheath at the boundary of a dusty plasma. *Physics of Plasmas*, *2*(4), 1343–1348.
30. Schweigert, I. V. (2015). Mode transition in miniature d.c. discharge driven by an auxiliary electrode. *Plasma Sources Science and Technology*, *24*(3), 034008.
31. Cram, L. E. (1983). A model of the cathode of a thermionic arc. *Journal of Physics D: Applied Physics*, *16*(9), 1643–1650.
32. Whipple, E. C. (1981). Potentials of surfaces in space. *Reports on Progress in Physics*, *44*(11), 1197–1250.
33. Komm, M., Ratynskaia, S., Tolias, P., Cavalier, J., Dejarnac, R., Gunn, J. P., & Podolnik, A. (2017). On thermionic emission from plasma-facing components in Tokamak-relevant conditions. *Plasma Physics and Controlled Fusion*, *59*(9), 094002.
34. Campanell, M. D., & Johnson, G. R. (2019). Thermionic cooling of the target plasma to a sub-eV temperature. *Physical Review Letters*, *122*(1), 015003.
35. Sorasio, G., Mendis, D. A., & Rosenberg, M. (2001). The role of thermionic emission in meteor physics. *Planetary and Space Science*, *49*(13), 1257–1264.
36. Poppe, A., Halekas, J. S., & Horányi, M. (2011). Negative potentials above the day-side lunar surface in the terrestrial plasma sheet: Evidence of non-monotonic potentials. *Geophysical Research Letters*, *38*(2).
37. Delzanno, G. L., & Tang, X.Z. (2014). Charging and heat collection by a positively charged dust grain in a plasma. *Physical Review Letters*, *113*(3), 035002.

38. Autricque, A., Khrapak, S. A., Couëdel, L., Fedorczak, N., Arnas, C., Layet, J.-M., & Grisolia, C. (2018). Electron collection and thermionic emission from a spherical dust grain in the space-charge limited regime. *Physics of Plasmas, 25*(6), 063701.
39. Kemp, R. F., & Sellen, J. M. (1966) Plasma Potential Measurements by Electron Emissive Probes. *Review of Scientific Instruments, 37*(4), 455–461.
40. Sheehan, J. P., Kaganovich, I. D., Wang, H., Sydorenko, D., Raitses, Y., & Hershkowitz, N. (2014). Effects of emitted electron temperature on the plasma sheath. *Physics of Plasmas, 21*(6), 063502.
41. Sheehan, J. P., Barnat, E. V., Weatherford, B. R., Kaganovich, I. D., & Hershkowitz, N. (2014). Emissive sheath measurements in the afterglow of a radio frequency plasma. *Physics of Plasmas, 21*(1), 013510.
42. Campanell, M. D., Khrabrov, A. V., & Kaganovich, I. D. (2012). Absence of Debye sheaths due to secondary electron emission. *Physical Review Letters, 108*(25), 255001.
43. Langendorf, S., & Walker, M. (2015). Effect of secondary electron emission on the plasma sheath. *Physics of Plasmas, 22*(3), 033515.
44. Sydorenko, D., Kaganovich, I., Raitses, Y., & Smolyakov, A. (2009). Breakdown of a space charge limited regime of a sheath in a weakly collisional plasma bounded by walls with secondary electron emission. *Physical Review Letters, 103*(14), 145004.
45. Ahedo, E. (2002). Presheath/sheath model with secondary electron emission from two parallel walls. *Physics of Plasmas, 9*(10), 4340–4347.
46. Griskey, M. C., & Stenzel, R. L. (1999). Secondary-electron-emission instability in a plasma. *Physical Review Letters, 82*(3), 556–559.
47. Chen, F. F. (1984). *Introduction to plasma physics and controlled fusion, 1*. Plenum Press.
48. Nakamura, Y., & Sarma, A. (2001). Observation of ion-acoustic solitary waves in a dusty plasma. *Physics of Plasmas, 8*(9), 3921–3926.

CHAPTER 4

SCATTERING CROSS-SECTION OF CHARGED DUST PARTICLES IN MAGNETIZED PLASMA

4.1. INTRODUCTION

Studies of charged dust particles in plasma in recent decades are getting importance due to their relevance to applications in semiconductor industry and chip manufacturing, and other various space exploration applications. Until the 1980s, dust particles were considered an impurity in plasma etching and processing of chip manufacturing processes. Ikezi (1986) first found out the growth of dust inside the plasma system and proposed that micrometres size particles might show the process of Coulomb crystallization [1]. After this discovery, there have been several experiments regarding the study of charged dust particles in plasma and its various structure formation in the laboratory plasma [2-8]. Parallel to the experimental, insightful research towards the computational method such as particle-in-cell (PIC) simulation, COMSOL, PlasmaPy and other open-source packages, has made progress in understanding the fundamental behavior of charged dust particles along with the plasma species [9-13]. Nevertheless, the theoretical understanding of dusty plasma is limited, and at the same time, the numerical analysis of dust particle interactions in magnetized plasma systems have not been explored much.

Throughout the decades, significant studies have involved in various diagnostics of laboratory plasma systems. Most common method is employed by inserting the probe into the plasma system and corresponding I-V curve obtained from the probe is used for measurement of plasma parameters. These plasma parameters describe the best possible way for the confinement of plasma. Charging mechanism of probes is understood by OML theory, through which plasma parameters are generally measured. Orbital motion limited (OML) theory describes the probe theory where electrons and ions are collected by the probe and acquires a floating potential in plasma systems. Similarly, the dust particles charging mechanism can be understood by OML theory. Electron and ion currents can be derived from the well-established OML theory, which is valid for current investigation [14-19]. Primarily, it deals with the collisionless of electrons and ions near the particle orbit, which is appropriate in dusty plasma cases where the mean free path (λ_{mfp}) is much larger than the particle size [20]. The OML theory postulates, for example, that dust particles only absorb plasma particles whose impact parameters are equal to or smaller than those at which the dust particle is touched tangentially. On the other hand, dust particles do not absorb plasma particles whose impact parameters are larger than this critical value. This assumption is used in this chapter and more brief explanation with theory is given in [21]. However, Allen-Boyd-Reynolds (ABR) and Bernstein-Rabinowitz-Laframboise (BRL) are the other probe theories that also describe the probe's charging mechanism, where BRL theory greatly overestimates the plasma density, while the ABR theory underestimates it [22]. Therefore, the OML theory is the best describes the charging mechanism of probes. Magnetic field (B) has become an essential part of the confinement of plasmas in tokamaks, stellarators, and so on [23-24]. Therefore, theoretical, and experimental research in magnetized plasma and magnetized dusty plasma becomes important to investigate. Charged plasma species ($\alpha = e, i$) in external magnetic fields change their trajectories as they circulate around the field lines. Hence, the introduction of **B** makes plasma anisotropic and collisional. As **B** increases, the Larmor radius of charged species reduces. Conventionally, plasma or dusty plasma becomes magnetized when the ion Larmor radius becomes less than the characteristic length of the plasma system. Due to these perturbations, the charging mechanism of dust particles is modified. One cannot simply assume the spherical symmetry of potential around the particle in anisotropic plasma. However, deviations from the spherical symmetry on the particle charge have not been purely estimated [25].

In this chapter, the influence of **B** on the interaction of charged dust particles and the scattering cross-section of the same is studied numerically and simulation by using COMSOL Multiphysics Software. Charged dust particles interact through the potential developed across dust particles from the balance of electron and ion currents. Thus, dust-dust scatters through this developed potential and measurement of this scattering cross-section are the main motive of this work. The effect of **B** on the change in scattering cross-section is observed in few experimental conditions [26-29]. Yukawa potential is considered and surface potential of charged dust particles is derived by considering the effect of drift velocity in velocity equation. The effect of **B** is evaluated through kinematics of plasma species charging the dust particles. Theoretically, various efforts have been made [30-31] to understand the nature of the current collection by dust particles or probes in presence of **B**, but no such generalized solution has been developed since the complexity level of solving equations becomes more rigorous and tedious. Trajectories of both electrons and ions change in the presence of **B** as they circulate around magnetic field lines and their corresponding velocity distribution becomes anisotropic around the dust particles. This change in the path of electrons and ions significantly affects dust-dust interaction by a change in accumulation of charge on the surface of dust particles and hence, change in scattering cross-section. The velocity of charged dust particles derived from Lorenz's law and collection currents derived from the Maxwellian distribution function have been considered. The Plasma Module of COMSOL Multiphysics simulation software is used to simulate charged dust particles in the presence of ***B***.

4.2. BRIEF REVIEW OF PREVIOUS WORK

From prediction of dust crystals [1] to observation in laboratory experiments to astrophysical phenomena, the basic concept underlying in dusts in plasma has become utmost for many applications. The generation of dust crystals was detected experimentally in a high-frequency discharge near the bottom electrode at the boundary of the near-cathode region [32-34]. Fortov *et al.*, observed the dust crystal in strata of glow discharge plasma [35]. One of the biggest advantages of these dust crystals is it can be observed through naked eye by illuminating laser light on dust particle. GE Morfill did the first experimental observation of dust crystals in a RF plasma with 7 µm diameter of dust particles in a weakly ionized argon plasma [36]. Fortov *et al.* also observed the dust crystals in DC glow discharge plasma, atmospheric plasma, and nuclear induced dusty plasma [2, 3, 37]. Fortov *et al.*, Lipaev *et al.*, and Nefedov *et al.* produced the dust particles structures in dc glow discharge plasma [35, 38, 39]. Vasilyak *et al.*, presented dust structures in long conical tubes forming different layers with varying mass, size and charge. These structures are depended on pressure and current of the conical discharge tube [40].

After the prediction and observation of dust crystals in both RF and DC plasma, it became a hot topic in recent decades for investigation. Dust does acts as a contamination in all the earth-based experiments only because of its scale length compared to the plasma species (ions & electrons). In some practical applications of plasma, dust cloud formation is inevitable and undesirable, such as plasma etching and coating of thin films. Due to its scale length, charged dust particles becomes important to study in terms of its complexity and instabilities in plasma. However, most of the times dusty plasma was considered for the study of cosmological events, planetary and cometary atmospheres, planet formation, interstellar medium etc., [41-43]. Juan *et al.* showed how dust clusters structures are formed with the increase of number of dust particles in gradual manner. The phase transition of dust particles in plasma is also an interesting part where RF or DC power manipulates the dust crystal formation and melting [44]. Thomas and Morfill; Morfill *et al.*, observed that with increasing RF power, number density of plasma species increases and hence decrease in Debye length. Therefore, distance between dust particle decreases and dust cloud starts shrinking. Authors showed that with change in pressure inside the chamber, the dust structures could be manipulated accordingly [45-46].

Researchers got more intrigued on how charged dust particles act in an external force or in a force field. Such forces can be used for ordering, spatial movements and change in dynamics of plasma experiments. One of the primary and external force is magnetic field used for the confinement of plasma in a Tokamak, Stellarators and fusion devices. Presence of external magnetic field (***B***) (most of them are ***B*** = 400 G) has larger influence on charged dust particles such as rotation of dust particles and change in the structure of dust clouds with varying ***B*** [47-54]. Sato *et al.*, performed the dusty plasma experiment at ***B*** = 4 T in a RF plasma and stated the difficulties of studies dust clouds in DC discharge plasma [27]. Vasil'ev *et al.*, performed the experiment in stratified DC glow discharge plasma with axial ***B*** = 2500 G to study the effect of B on dust structures such as oscillations of dust particles, angular velocity, dust structures etc., [55]. Further, dust particles can be created during magnetron sputtering process of various materials such as titanium, copper, graphite, silicon etc. [56-60].

Over the past few years, there is large number of interests in experimental studies of magnetized dusty plasma with and without external magnetic field [61-68]. Yet, there has been less significant work in theoretical description of dusty plasma and understanding the physics behind the dust clouds. It has been determined through experimentation that the presence of a regular crystalline structure is a fact, and it is feasible to center one's attention on an interpretation of the results of this investigation.

4.3. MATHEMATICAL MODELLING

In the present work, weakly ionized plasma in uniform and externally applied static magnetic fields is considered. Spherical dust particles having radius r_d are introduced into the plasma system. Particle surfaces acquire charges ($-q$, $+q$) and rest in a floating potential (φ_{fp}). φ_{fp} can be found out from the balance of electron and ion currents to the particle derived from the OML theory by assuming collisionless (as discussed in previous section, where mean free path is larger than compared to system length) and isotropic plasma. The current density of the plasma species ($\alpha = e, i$) absorbed by the particle surface is given by the integral equation [27] as

$$j_\alpha = q \int v \, \sigma_\alpha(q,v) f(v_\alpha) dv \qquad (4.1)$$

where $f(v_\alpha)$ can be found out from the Maxwellian velocity distribution function given as

$$f(v_\alpha) = \frac{4\pi v_\alpha^2}{(\sqrt{\pi}\theta)^3} exp\left(\frac{-v_\alpha^2}{\theta^2}\right) \qquad (4.2)$$

θ is the velocity vector of electrons and ions under the influence of Lorentz force and is expressed as a function of time

$$\theta(t) = \Omega_{c\alpha} \times r_{c\alpha} + \frac{\vec{E}_\perp \times \vec{B}}{B^2} + \frac{q\vec{E}_\parallel t}{m_\alpha} + v_\parallel(0) \qquad (4.3)$$

where, $\Omega_{c\alpha}=|q|B/m_\alpha$ and $r_{c\alpha} = m_\alpha v_\alpha/|q|B$ is the gyrofrequency and gyro radius of plasma species along the magnetic field. $v_{\parallel}(0)$ is the thermal velocities of electrons and ions given by $v_{t\alpha} = \sqrt{3T_\alpha/m_\alpha}$ at time $t = 0$s. T_α and m_α are the temperature and mass of the plasma species respectively. Two components of electric field $E_\parallel$

and $E_\perp$ has been considered for diffusion of electrons and ions through parallel and perpendicular to **B** as shown in Eqn. (4.3). The effect of **B** on electrons is quicker than ions since ions are heavier than electrons. The charging of dust particles at lower **B** is relatively small, because the gyro-radius of electrons is larger than the size of the dust particles. Electron current to the dust particle is reduced and ion current does not change substantially. As **B** increases, electron gyro-radius (r_{ce}) reduces and at a certain **B**, it becomes equal to the size of the dust particles and increasing the intensity of electrons to the surface of charged dust particles. From Eqn. (4.3), it can be shown that at **B** = 0, the particle's velocity equation shows thermal velocity. To evaluate Eqn. (4.1), it is important to calculate the value of σ_α foremost. σ_α is the absorption cross section and can be derived from the conservation of energy and momentum of plasma species absorbing on the dust particles.

$$\sigma_\alpha = \pi r_d^2 \left(1 + \frac{2q\varphi_{fp}}{m_\alpha \theta_\alpha^2}\right) \quad (4.4)$$

Integral of Eqn. (4.1) can now be resolved from Eqn. (4.2), (4.3) and (4.4) and we can write currents to the particle surface for electrons and ions as,

$$I_e = -4\sqrt{\pi} q r_d^2 n_{e0} \theta_e \exp(q\varphi_{fp}/T_e) \quad (4.5)$$

$$I_i = 4\sqrt{\pi} q r_d^2 n_{i0} \theta_i (1 - q\varphi_{fp}/T_i) \quad (4.6)$$

n_{eo} and n_{io} are the electron and ion equilibrium plasma densities. From the balance of electron and ion currents, φ_{fp} can be expressed as

$$\varphi_{fp} = \frac{\delta(\zeta - 1)}{q} \quad (4.7)$$

where $\delta = T_e T_i / (T_i + T_e \zeta)$ and $\zeta = \theta_i/\theta_e$ are given respectively.

The classical treatment of potential has generally been expressed as proportional to $1/r^2$. The problem for estimating potential around the dust particles in various conditions considering their dependence of $1/r^3$, has been studied extensively by the physicists over the years and is available in the literature [69]. One of the widely and vividly accepted potential around the dust particle is the

Yukawa potential ($\varphi(r)$). However, the mathematical expression for the potential varies from one plasma system to another [70-76]. Poisson's equations can be solved through numerical analysis carried out with proper boundary conditions. It was observed that Yukawa potential around the dust particle could deviate or have asymptotic behaviour. However, the scattering phenomena of dust particles is not affected by any small deviations of potential around the dust particles [77]. Yukawa's potential for the charged dust particles is given as

$$\varphi(r) = r_d \frac{\varphi_{fp}}{r} exp\left(\frac{-r}{\lambda}\right) \quad (4.8)$$

where $\lambda \sim \lambda_d = \sqrt{(\lambda_{de}^2 \lambda_{di}^2 / \lambda_{de}^2 + \lambda_{di}^2)}$ and $\lambda_{de,i} = \sqrt{(\varepsilon_0 T_{e,i}/q^2 n_0)}$ is the effective screening length, $\varphi_d < 0$ for attraction and $\varphi_d > 0$ repulsion. $\lambda_{de,i}$ is the Debye radius of electron and ions, $T_{e,i,d}$ is the temperature of electron, ion and dust particle, respectively and n_0 is the undisturbed plasma density. Any types of collision between plasma electrons and ions have been neglected. The collisions between charged dust particles as two elastic bodies are considered as a binary collision, which works well in weakly ionized plasma. For binary interactions of the charged dust particles, impact parameter (b) and scattering angle (χ), are interdependent to each other which can be calculated as [78]

$$\chi(\rho) = \pi - 2b \int_{r_m}^{\infty} \left(\frac{dr}{r^2 \psi(r)}\right) \quad (4.9)$$

where, $\psi(r)$ is effective potential energy expressed as

$$\psi(r) = \left[1 - \frac{e\varphi(r)}{\varepsilon} - \frac{b^2}{r^2}\right]^{\frac{1}{2}} \quad (4.10)$$

r_m is distance of closest approach, which indicates that after this point however may be the attraction between particles, there is not much further penetration in the central field force of particles as $r \to 0$, ψ becomes infinite, and if $r \gg r_m$, the particle goes to infinity, and is evaluated by putting $\psi(r) = 0$;

$$r_m = b\left[1 - \frac{2\varphi(r_m)}{mv^2}\right]^{\frac{-1}{2}} \qquad (4.11)$$

Substituting the potential from Eqn. (4.8) in Eqn. (4.11), r_m is numerically solved and expressed as

$$r_m = \left[\left(\frac{b^2 b_0^2 \lambda^2}{4} - \left(\frac{b}{3} + \frac{bb_0}{3}\right)^3\right)^{\frac{1}{2}} - \frac{1}{2}bb_0\lambda\right]^{\frac{1}{3}} + \frac{\left(\frac{b}{3} + \frac{bb_0}{3}\right)}{\left[\left(\frac{b^2 b_0^2 \lambda^2}{4} - \left(\frac{b}{3} + \frac{bb_0}{3}\right)^3\right)^{\frac{1}{2}} - \frac{1}{2}bb_0\lambda\right]^{\frac{1}{3}}} \qquad (4.12)$$

where, $b_0 = 2\varphi_{fp}r_d/m_d v_d^2 \lambda$, m_d is the mass of the dust particle and velocity of dust particles $v_d \approx \sqrt{(T_d/m_d)}$, T_d is temperature of dust particle is assumed to be the same as ion temperature T_i. So, scattering cross-section is expressed in terms of χ and b as

$$\sigma = 2\pi \int_0^\infty (1 - cos(\chi)) b \, db \qquad (4.13)$$

Analysis of the above equation is extensively complicated and can be solved numerically, which is rigorous and time consuming. As can be seen from the Eqn. (4.12), which is derived for the current mathematical modelling, where distance of closest approach (r_m) is the limit of integration of Eqn. (4.9). In addition, impact parameter and scattering angle are strongly correlated to each other, which becomes lengthy and time-consuming problem to numerically solve. Therefore, introduction of the scattering parameter (β) i.e., ratio of coulomb radius to screening length of dust particles, which describes the strength of interaction between dust particles [78-81]. From Eqn. (4.8), a dimensionless parameter can be derived as $\beta = \varphi_{fp}/mv^2\lambda$. This can be seen from the effective potential energy Eqn. (4.10), such as if we normalize b and r with screening length (λ), then $\psi(r)$ only depends on parameter β. Similarly, dependence of β for scattering angle (χ) in (4.9) can be seen. From Eqn. (4.13), normalized σ/λ is also dependent on β. From Eqn. (4.10) and (4.8),

$$\psi(r) \approx \left[1 - \frac{e\beta r_d \exp\left(\frac{-r}{\lambda}\right)}{\lambda r}\right]^{\frac{1}{2}} \quad (4.14)$$

For a typical gas discharge plasma, such as $T_e/T_i = 10\sim100$, $r_d/\lambda \sim 10^{-1}\sim10^{-2}$, the value of $\beta \sim 0.3$-30. For the dust-dust particle interaction, β is derived depending on the size of the dust particle and floating potential, and β is rewritten as

$$\beta = \frac{\varphi_{fp} q r_d}{T_d \lambda_d} \quad (4.15)$$

For the value of $\beta << 1$, standard Coulomb scattering justifies and fails for $\beta >> 1$. Because the interaction of dust particle potential can be well present for $b>\lambda$, so the maximum impact parameter is revised to the distance of the closest approach. From the well-established, classical Coulomb scattering theory, scattering cross-section of the dust particles for maximum impact parameter (r_m (b_{max}) = λ) can be written in terms of the scattering parameter β as [81]

$$\sigma_{sc} = 4\pi \lambda_d^2 \beta^2 \ln\left(1 + \frac{1}{\beta}\right) \quad (4.16)$$

This procedure is not rigorous and monotonous, but it agrees with the present work and will be helpful for the computational studies. The problem of interaction of dust particles and estimating the scattering cross-section from the velocity profile of the dust particles is modelled in the COMSOL environment. The more detailed simulation setup is discussed in the next section.

4.4. SIMULATION SETUP

COMSOL multi-physics is a simulation software allowing an environment for modelling physics and engineering problems. Plasma module is one of the application modules, which models only low temperature discharge plasmas. It is a system, which involves fluid mechanics, statistical mechanics & thermodynamics, electromagnetics, heat and mass transfer. Plasma module provides almost all kinds of discharges such as inductively coupled plasmas (ICP), direct current discharges, capacitively coupled plasmas (CCP), microwave plasmas and corona discharges. Plasma module is the built-in interface for modeling low temperature plasma with the help of static or varying electric field. These interfaces define their own sets of domain equations, initial conditions, boundary conditions, predefined meshes, and predefined studies with solver settings for steady and transient analyses. In addition, plasma module gives the derived values and predefined plots. Poisson's equation can be used to solve transport equations for all types of species, including electrons, ions, and neutrals, in a self-consistent manner. Collisional properties of electrons with background gas can be calculated by mean energy equation gained by electric field.

For non-equilibrium discharges, the mean free path must be smaller than the usual reactor size. Low temperature (< 50eV) and weakly ionized, i.e., ion mass fraction must be less than around 1%. In this case, non-collision plasma requires a particle in cell (PIC) code. Methodologies involved in simulating plasma are fluid, kinetic and hybrid (fluid and kinetic) models. The fluid model is used by solving transport equations and assuming an electron energy distribution function (EEDF). The kinetic model is a particle-based model, taking the distribution of velocities of the particles. In comparison, a hybrid model is used involving a mixed fluid/kinetic model approach with particle and mesh based PDEs. The fluid approach treats all species as continuous media that can be characterized by macroscopic quantities such as the temperature. After that, the transport equations are solved for each species. Kinetic modelling can give accurate results, but its computer intensive means a lot of computational time is required and would be considered in future. The hybrid model limits the computational requirement. For fluid approach in plasma simulating, at least we need 4 PDEs and transport equations to be used for electron density transport, electron energy density transport, Poisson's equations for electrostatics, and which is given as

$$\rho \left[\frac{\partial \vec{v}}{\partial t} + (\vec{v}.\nabla)\vec{v}\right] = qn(\vec{E} + \vec{v} \times \vec{B}) - \vec{\nabla}p \qquad (4.17)$$

$$\frac{\partial \rho}{\partial t} + \nabla.(\rho\vec{v}) = 0 \qquad (4.18)$$

$$\nabla.\vec{E} = \frac{q}{\varepsilon_0}(n_i - n_e - Z_d n_d) \qquad (4.19)$$

where ρ is the mass density of the plasma species (electrons & ions), $n_{i,e,d}$ is the number density of the ions, electrons and dust particles and p is the pressure of the plasma gas. In addition to the plasma module, if any other physics phenomena want to understand, AC/DC module, RF module and Particle tracing module is also incorporated. Being a true finite element code, one can introduce quadratic, cubic, and greater basis functions. COMSOL is less computationally intensive and relatively easy to use. In the present COMSOL simulation program, simple laboratory scale DC discharge plasma is considered in the presence of magnetic fields and as shown in Fig. 4.1(a). Plasma is created between the two electrodes; the upper electrode acts as anode and the lower electrode as cathode. Effect of collision frequency has also been considered for the whole set of computation. Magnetic field is applied in the negative z-axis parallel to the electric field.

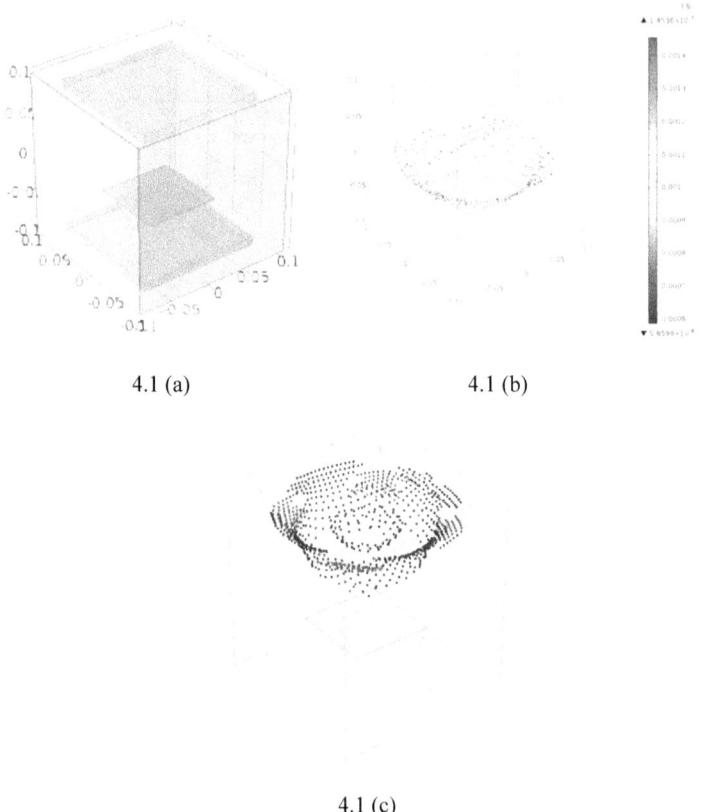

4.1 (a)   4.1 (b)

4.1 (c)

Fig. 4.1 A typical laboratory scale setup at $B = 0$ T and $E = 20$ V in DC discharge conditions with different time. (a) Simulation setup (b) $t = 0.5$ s and (c) $t = 2$ s. Electrode is kept in the XY plane and vertical direction of the chamber is the Z-axis.

A plane is defined parallel to the XY plane at different time intervals to calculate the diameter of the scattering cross-section of charged dust grains. XY plane is also the plane of electrodes kept and vertical chamber is the Z-axis. Magnetic field variations are kept between 0.25 T to 6 T to study the effect of weak to strong magnetization on charged species. Electrodes are kept at 20 cm apart and dust particles of size 5 μm are placed on the bottom electrode. The experimental plasma parameters considered for the simulation processes are as: $n_i = n_e \sim 10^{12}\ m^{-3}$, $T_e = 1$ eV, $T_i = 0.1$ eV $= T_d$. The dust dispenser is placed 5 cm above the bottom electrode. The charge gained by the dust particles in the presence of plasma is considered as $10^3\ Q$. The effective mass of dust is considered as 1.2×10^{-17} kg. All the simulation is continued for a time frame between 0.5 s to 2 s. Both inner and outer points of charged dust grains coagulation are considered. For all simulations, XY is considered as the plane of electrodes. Colour bar on the right-hand side shows the velocity profile of the charged dust grains. This velocity profile is used in calculating scattering cross-section of same. The velocity component, which is not parallel to the magnetic field, will gyrate along the field lines with more confinement toward the centre.

4.5. RESULTS AND DISCUSSION

Current work will help the theoretical understanding of charged dust particles in the presence of an external magnetic field. With initiation of plasma inside the DC plasma system, the dust particles levitate from the bottom electrode by acquiring charges and attain floating potential, which is given by balancing the force due to gravity (F_g) and applied electric field (F_E), such as $F_g = F_E$. Fig. 4.1 shows the charge dust particles distribution levitated at $\boldsymbol{B} = 0$ T and at an applied electric field $\boldsymbol{E} = 20$ V. Fig. 4.1(b) shows the charged dust particle distribution for $t = 0.5$ s simulation time. If simulation time is increased to 2 s, Fig. 4.1(c) shows the tendency of particles moving towards the upper electrode (anode). Velocity profile of electron or negative dust particles seem to have a symmetry profile as can be seen from Fig. 4.1(c). Electric field force at which dust particles levitate is considered as a critical electric field and has been maintained the same throughout the experiment, with varying $\boldsymbol{B}$. Critical electric field $\boldsymbol{E_c} = 6$ V, at which charged dust particles levitate above the bottom electrode is established as shown in Fig. 4.2 with dust particles dispersed comprehensively. From the velocity distribution of charged dust particles, at $\boldsymbol{B} = 0$ T, the energy of dust particles is low. Hence, there is weak interaction between the charged dust particles. Keeping E_c constant, dust particle collisions are studied under the influence of increasing B. With increase in B, dust particles agglomerate towards the center and start moving to the upper electrode as shown in Fig. 4.3. Magnetization of electrons and ions in this experiment begins when the value of B changes from 0.25 T to 1 T, and in this case one can calculate from $r_{ca} = r_d$. Higher B results in dust particles agglomerating towards the center. In both the cases, Fig. 4.3(a) and 4.3(b), simulation-running time is kept at 0.5s.

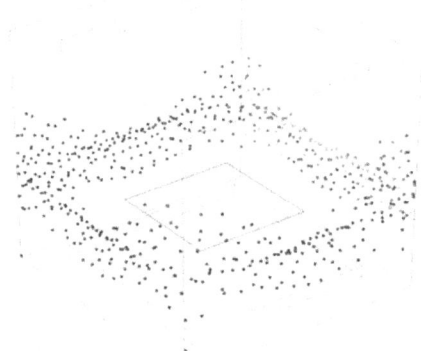

Fig. 4.2 Simulation results for the movement of charged dust particles at $E_c = 6$ V and $B = 0$ T for $t = 0.5$ s

Rotation of dust particles is observed in Fig. 4.3(a). At higher magnetic fields, electrons are magnetized and gyrate along the magnetic field, hence concentrating the electrons towards the center of the plasma system. Electro-negative dust particles also tend to become tightly bound as in Fig. 4.3(b) forming a multi-layer structure instead of a single layer structure as in Fig. 4.3(a). In Fig. 4.4(a), simulation-running time is kept at 0.5 s and dust particles are observed inside the system in well-defined stacks.

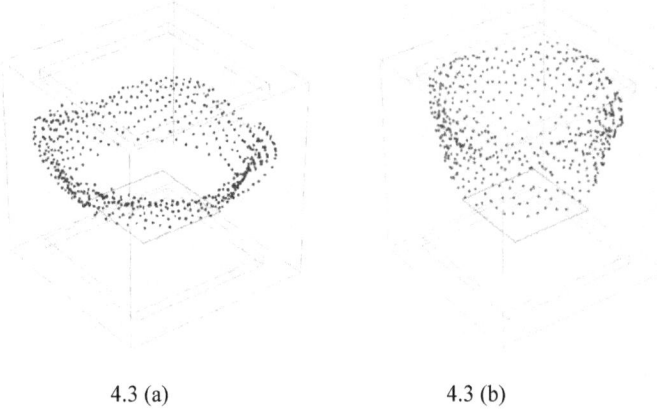

4.3 (a)   4.3 (b)

Fig. 4.3 Spreading of charged dust particles between the electrodes at (a) $B = 0.25$ T and (b) $B = 1$ T, for the simulation time 0.5 s. Positional change of a particle with time is shown vertically.

Fig. 4.3(b) and 4.4(a) clearly show that with the increasing magnetic fields, magnetization of charged particles makes them act in a more collective approach and overall confinement becomes more effective within the electrodes. Highly energetic electrons do not reach the surface of the dust particles, and as a result, depletion of electrons in dust cloud sheath tends to attract surrounding dust particles to maintain the equilibrium. In these two cases, unlike at $B = 0.25$ T, charged dust particles span throughout the length of electrodes but with more confinement. However, at $B = 0.25$ T, particles are shifting toward the upper electrode and making it almost circular in shape. At higher B value, charged dusts remain throughout the length of electrodes and are observed as cylindrical in shape with the creation of few concentric circles. Positioning of dust charged particles in this case resembles them almost like an amorphous crystal. However, complete physical understanding of the same requires more investigation in future works. When B is increased further as shown in Fig. 4.4 (b) and 4.4 (c), the dust particles try to form a parabolic shape and the particles rotate about their axis but are not able to scatter further. Very few dust particles with less energetic electrons remain in the lower part of the electrodes and enhance the confinement significantly. The scattering cross-section of charged dust grains both in absence and presence of magnetic fields have been estimated with relative error as shown in Fig. 4.5 and measured relative to the change in position of dust particles. From the Fig. 4.3 and 4.4, it is observed that charged dust forms a circular pattern.

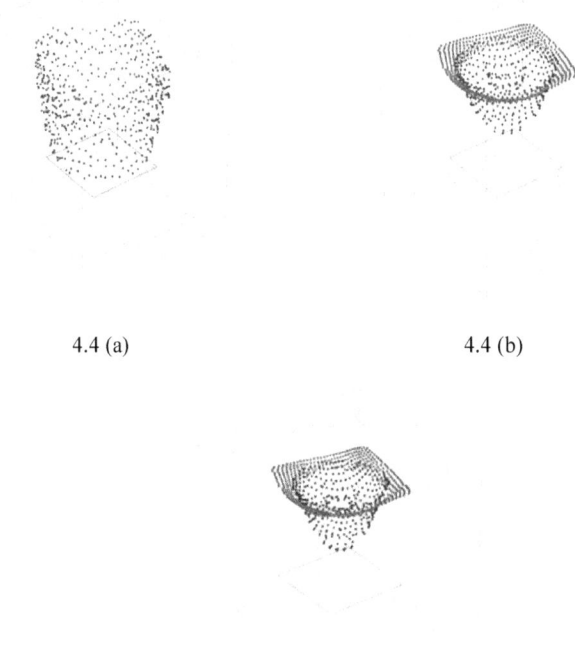

4.4 (a)   4.4 (b)

4.4 (c)

Fig. 4.4 Behavioral changes of charged dust grains between the electrode at (a) B = 2 T, t = 0.5 s, (b) B = 4 T, t = 1 min and (c) B = 6 T, t =1 min. Positional change of a particle with time is shown vertically.

For the calculation of scattering cross-section, inner point and outer point of the dust cloud structure has been taken. Comparatively, the inner point has a smaller scattering cross-section to the outer point as seen from Fig. 4.5. It is observed that the scattering cross-section is decreasing with an increasing magnetic field. There is an exponential decrease in the value of scattering cross-section, for the value of **B** from 0 to 2 T. This can be associated with the magnetization of electrons, and confinement of charge dust particles. On further increase of **B** from 2 T to 6 T, there is not much change in the value of scattering cross-section. The charge dust particles tend to form a single layer structure from multi-layer structure as seen in Fig. 4.4(b) and 4.4(c).

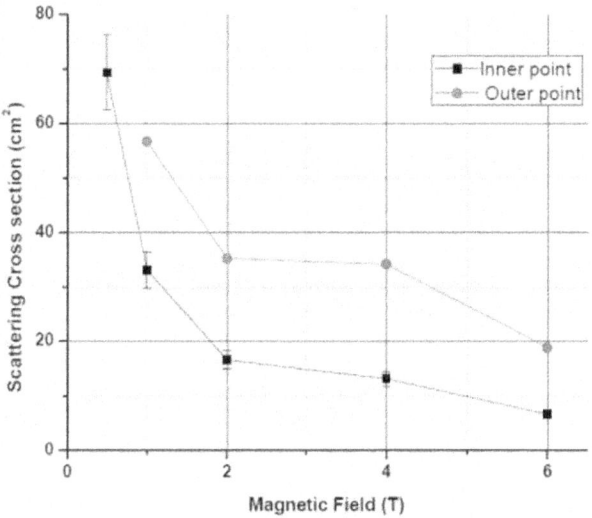

Fig. 4.5 Scattering cross-section of dust particles at inner and outer point of the dust particle distribution from COMSOL.

Considering the same computational analysis plasma parameter, numerical equations have been solved in terms of **B**. Eqn. (4.16) shows the dependence of scattering cross-section on the scattering parameter β. Whereas, β is calculated from the Eqn. (4.15), which is directly proportional to φ_{fp}. All the other parameters in the

Eqn. (4.15) are kept constant ($r_d = 5$ mm, $T_d = T_i = 0.1$ eV) and φ_{fp} can be evaluated from the Eqn. (4.7) with varying $\boldsymbol{B}$. φ_{fp} is derived from the collection of electrons and ions in the presence of magnetic field from the Eqn. (4.5) and (4.6). Under the influence of the magnetic fields, the velocity vector of electrons and ions has components perpendicular and parallel to the magnetic field. Considering these two components in the velocity vector, Eqn. (4.3) is derived from Lorenz's law and the collection current is estimated. Fig. 4.6, corresponds to the floating potential of charged dust particles with increasing $\boldsymbol{B}$ and $\zeta = \theta_i/\theta_e$ i.e., ratio of cyclotron velocities. Cyclotron frequency $(\Omega_{c\alpha})$ is normalized to plasma frequency $(\omega_{p\alpha} = \sqrt{n_\alpha q^2/m_\alpha \varepsilon_0})$. It is observed that, floating potential exponentially decreases with increasing $\boldsymbol{B}$. Similarly, ζ decreases with increase in $\boldsymbol{B}$.

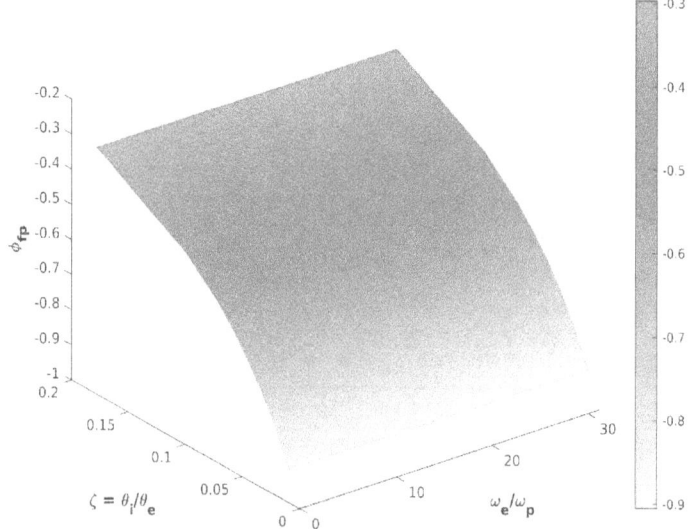

Fig. 4.6 Floating potential of dust particles with increasing $\boldsymbol{B}$ for $T_e = 1$ eV and $T_i = 0.1$ eV.

At lower **B**, the electron does not reach to the dust particle surface since the gyro radius of the electron is much larger than the collection radius of dust particle i.e., $r_{ca} > r_d$, hence lower accumulation of charge by dust particles. As $r_{ca} \approx r_d$ satisfies, only higher energy electrons tend to reach the dust particle surface. Lower electron energy reflects from the charged dust particle surface and consequently not much further increase in φ_{fp}. From the Eqn. (4.6), the graph obtained for scattering cross-section with **B** is given in Fig. 4.7. Scattering cross-section decreases with increase in **B** as shown computationally in Fig. 4.5 and numerically in Fig. 4.7. Depletion of charge collection by the dust particles surface weakens the interaction potential and thus enables the interaction of dust particles with the nearest dust particle. Therefore, the Yukawa potential considered between charged dust particles is a good approximation. Interaction is characterized mainly by the collection of electrons and ions on dust particles. φ_{fp} is implicitly expressed in terms of **B** incorporated in the velocity distribution of electrons and ions.

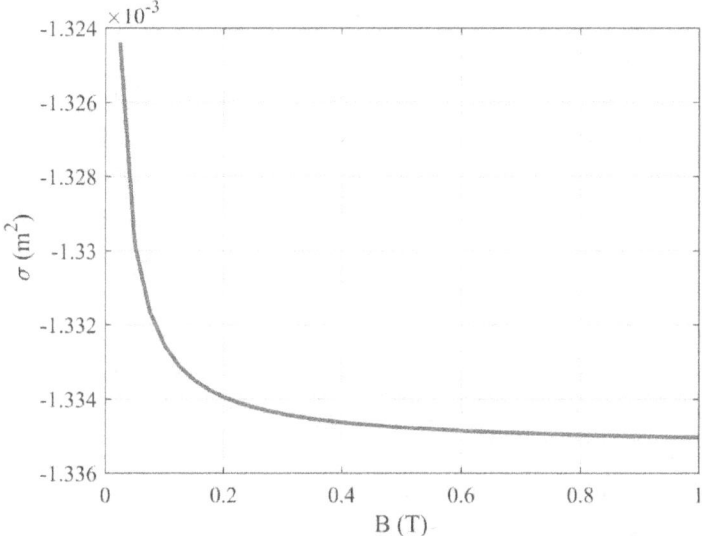

Fig. 4.7 Scattering cross-section of dust particles in terms of β w.r.t **B**.

4.6. CONCLUSION

Interaction of charged dust-dust particles in the presence of externally applied magnetic fields has been studied numerically and computationally. Parallel and perpendicular velocity vector components of electrons and ions have been included in the velocity distribution function. Floating potential (φ_{fp}) of charged dust particles and total velocity vector for electrons and ions is derived in the presence of a magnetic field. The complexity of the integration involving distance of the closest approach (r_m) as one of the limits in solving the scattering angle is tedious and requires more than one solution numerically. Contrary, r_m implicitly depends on B and too many variables to resolve the equation. So, the scattering parameter (β) becomes useful in solving the scattering cross-section, as it is proportional to φ_{fp}. With the help of β, the scattering cross-section given in Eqn. (4.16), is derived in approximation of r_m (b_{max}) = λ. Fig. 4.7, shows the scattering cross-section decreasing with increase in magnetic field. At lower B, the gyro radius of plasma species is greater than the size of the dust particles ($r_{ca} > r_d$), thus reducing currents of electrons and ions to the dust particle surface. This leads to depletion of charge accumulation by the dust particle and increasing the tendency to gain electrons from nearby charged dust particles. Therefore, reducing the scattering cross-section of charged dust particles. At relatively higher B, electrons are magnetized and become $r_{ca} \approx r_d$. Therefore, only fast electrons or electrons with a significant amount of energy can reach the surface of the charged dust particle. Lower energy electrons are reflected from the charged dust particle. Similar results obtained for DC plasma system in COMSOL Multi-physics simulation software. Both Fig. 4.5 and 4.7 shows the same results of scattering cross-section. As seen from the curve in Fig. 4.5, scattering cross-section decreases with increasing B. Also observed from Fig. 4.3(b) and 4.3(a), at relatively higher B, i.e., near 2 T, multi-layer dust cloud structure is formed. Whereas at B = 6 T, the charge dust particles move towards the upper electrode and form a parabolic shape crystal with high rotational velocities observed in Fig. 4.4(c). Numerical and computational results of the charged dust particle in presence of B, has shown that scattering cross-section of charged dust particle decreases with increasing in B. Charged dust clouds forms a crystal-like structure at higher B. However, there is a still research gap in terms of the equation derived for the interaction potential of charged dust particles.

REFERENCES

1. Ikezi, H. (1986). Coulomb solid of small particles in plasmas. *Physics of Fluids*, *29*(6), 1764–1766.
2. Fortov, V. E., Nefedov, A. P., Petrov, O. F., Samarian, A. A., Chernyschev, A. V., & Lipaev, A. M. (February 1996). Experimental observation of Coulomb ordered structure in sprays of thermal dusty plasmas. *Journal of Experimental and Theoretical Physics Letters*, *63*(3), 187–192.
3. Fortov, V. E., Nefedov, A. P., Torchinskii, V. M., Molotkov, V. I., Khrapak, A. G., Petrov, O. F., & Volykhin, K. F. (1996). Crystallization of a dusty plasma in the positive column of a glow discharge. *Journal of Experimental and Theoretical Physics Letters*, *64*(2), 92–98.
4. Ishihara, O., Kamimura, T., Hirose, K. I., & Sato, N. (2002). Rotation of a two-dimensional Coulomb cluster in a magnetic field. *Physical Review E*, *66*(4), 046406.
5. Melzer, A., Klindworth, M., & Piel, A. (2001). Normal modes of 2D finite clusters in complex plasmas. *Physical Review Letters*, *87*(11, August), Art. no. 115002.
6. Sarma, A., & Nakamura, Y. (2009). Ion-acoustic shock waves with negative ions in presence of dust particulates. *Physics Letters A*, *373*(45), 4174–4177.
7. Morfill, G. E., Thomas, H. M., Konopka, U., Rothermel, H., Zuzic, M., Ivlev, A., & Goree, J. (1999). Condensed plasmas under microgravity. *Physical Review Letters*, *83*(8), 1598–1601.

8. Thomas, H., Morfill, G. E., Demmel, V., Goree, J., Feuerbacher, B., & Möhlmann, D. (1994). Plasma crystal: Coulomb crystallization in a dusty plasma. *Physical Review Letters, 73*(5), 652–655.
9. Hutchinson, I. H., & Patacchini, L. (2010). Flowing plasmas and absorbing objects: Analytic and numerical solutions culminating 80 years of ion collection theory. *Plasma Physics and Controlled Fusion, 52*(12, December), Art. no. 124005.
10. Patacchini, L., Hutchinson, I. H., & Lapenta, G. (2007). Electron collection by a negatively charged sphere in a collisionless magnetoplasma. *Physics of Plasmas, 14*(6), 062111.
11. Kim, H. C., Iza, F., Yang, S. S., Radmilovíc-Radjenovíc, M., & Lee, J. K. (2005). Particle and fluid simulations of low-temperature plasma discharges: Benchmarks and kinetic effects. *Journal of Physics D: Applied Physics, 38*(19), R283–R301.
12. Kushner, M. J. (2009). Hybrid modelling of low temperature plasmas for fundamental investigations and equipment design. *Journal of Physics D: Applied Physics, 42*(19), Art. no. 194013.
13. Verboncoeur, J. P. (2005). Particle simulation of plasmas: Review and advances. *Plasma Physics and Controlled Fusion, 47*(5), A231–A260.
14. Sanmartin, J. R. (1970). Theory of a probe in a strong magnetic field. *Physics of Fluids, 13*(1), 103–116.
15. Laframboise, J. G., & Rubinstein, J. (1976). Theory of a cylindrical probe in a collisionless magnetoplasma. *Physics of Fluids, 19*(12), 1900–1908.
16. Allen, J. E., Annaratone, B. M., & De Angelis, U. (2000). On the orbital motion limited theory for a small body at floating potential in a Maxwellian plasma. *Journal of Plasma Physics, 63*(4), 299–309.
17. Laframboise, J. G., & Sonmor, L. J. (1993). Current collection by probes and electrodes in space magnetoplasmas: A review. *Journal of Geophysical Research: Space Physics, 98*(A1), 337–357.

18. Allen, J. E. (1992). Probe theory–the orbital motion approach. *Physica Scripta*, *45*(5), 497–503.
19. Whipple, E. C. (1981). Potentials of surfaces in space. *Reports on Progress in Physics*, *44*(11), 1197–1250.
20. Tsytovich, V. N., Sato, N., & Morfill, G. E. (2003). Note on the charging and spinning of dust particles in complex plasmas in a strong magnetic field. *New Journal of Physics*, *5*, 43.
21. Tsytovich, V. N. (1997). Dust plasma crystals, drops, and clouds. *Physics-Uspekhi*, *40*(1), 53–94.
22. Chen, F. F., Evans, J. D., & Zawalski, W. (2012). Calibration of Langmuir probes against microwaves and plasma oscillation probes. *Plasma Sources Science and Technology*, *21*(5), Art. no. 055002.
23. Fortov, V. E., Ivlev, A. V., Khrapak, S. A., Khrapak, A. G., & Morfill, G. E. (2005). Complex (dusty) plasmas: Current status, open issues, perspectives. *Physics Reports*, *421*(1–2), 1–103.
24. Yaroshenko, V. V., Morfill, G. E., Samsonov, D., & Vladimirov, S. V. (2004). Agglomerations of magnetized dust particles in complex plasmas. *IEEE Transactions on Plasma Science*, *32*(2), 675–679.
25. Ignatov, A. M. (2005). Basics of dusty plasma. *Plasma Physics Reports*, *31*(1), 46–56.
26. Puttscher, M., & Melzer, A. (2014). Dust particles under the influence of crossed electric and magnetic fields in the sheath of an rf discharge. *Physics of Plasmas*, *21*(12), Art. no. 123704.
27. Sato, N., Uchida, G., Kaneko, T., Shimizu, S., & Iizuka, S. (2001). Dynamics of fine particles in magnetized plasmas. *Physics of Plasmas*, *8*(5), 1786–1790.
28. Kaw, P. K., Nishikawa, K., & Sato, N. (2002). Rotation in collisional strongly coupled dusty plasmas in a magnetic field. *Physics of Plasmas*, *9*(2), 387–390.

29. Samsonov, D., Zhdanov, S., Morfill, G., & Steinberg, V. (2003). Levitation and agglomeration of magnetic grains in a complex (dusty) plasma with magnetic field. *New Journal of Physics*, *5*, 24.
30. Salimullah, M., Sandberg, I., & Shukla, P. K. (2003). Dust charge fluctuations in a magnetized dusty plasma. *Physical Review E*, *68*(2), Art. no. 027403.
31. Sugawara, M. (1966). Electron probe current in a magnetized plasma. *Physics of Fluids*, *9*(4), 797–800.
32. Chu, J. H., & I, L. (1994). Direct observation of Coulomb crystals and liquids in strongly coupled rf dusty plasmas. *Physical Review Letters*, *72*(25), 4009–4012.
33. Melzer, A., Trottenberg, T., & Piel, A. (1994). Experimental determination of the charge on dust particles forming Coulomb lattices. *Physics Letters A*, *191*(3–4), 301–308.
34. Hayashi, Y., & Tachibana, S. (1994). Observation of Coulomb-crystal formation from carbon particles grown in a methane plasma. *Japanese Journal of Applied Physics*, *33*, L804–L806.
35. Fortov, V. E., Nefedov, A. P., Torchinsky, V. M., Molotkov, V. I., Petrov, O. F., Samarian, A. A., & Lipaev, A. M. (1997b). Crystalline structures of strongly coupled dusty plasmas in d.c. glow discharge strata. *Physics Letters A*, *229*(5), 317–322.
36. Morfill, G. E., & Thomas, H. (1996). Plasma crystal. *Journal of Vacuum Science and Technology A*, *14*(2), 490–495.
37. Fortov, V. E., Vladimirov, V. I., Deputatova, L. V., Molotkov, V. I., Nefedov, A. P., Rykov, V. A., Torchinskii, V. M., & Khudyakov, A. V. (1999). Ordered dusty structures in plasma produced by nuclear particles. *Doklady Physics*, *44*(5), 279–282. Pleiades Publishing Ltd.
38. Nefedov, A. P., Petrov, O. F., Molotkov, V. I., & Fortov, V. E. (2000). Formation of liquid like and crystalline structures in dusty plasmas. *Journal of Experimental and Theoretical Physics Letters*, *72*(4), 218–226.

39. Lipaev, A. M., Molotkov, V. I., Nefedov, A. P., Petrov, O. F., Torchinskii, V. M., Fortov, V. E., Khrapak, A. G., & Khrapak, S. A. (1997). Ordered structures in a non-ideal dusty glow-discharge plasma. *Journal of Experimental and Theoretical Physics*, *85*(6), 1110–1118.
40. Vasilyak, L. M., Vetchinin, S. P., Nefedov, A. P., & Polyakov, D. N. (2000). Ordered structures of microparticles in a glow discharge. *High Temperature*, *38*(5), 675–679.
41. Grün, E., Morfill, G. E., & Mendis, D. A. (1984). Dust-magnetosphere interactions. In R. Greenberg & A. Brahic (Eds.), *Planetary rings* (pp. 275–332). University Arizona Press.
42. Goertz, C. K. (1989). Dusty plasmas in the solar system. *Reviews of Geophysics*, *27*(2), 271–292.
43. Hartquist, T. W., Havnes, O., & Morfill, G. E. (1992). The effects of dust on the dynamics of astronomical and space plasmas. *Fundamentals of Cosmic Physics*, *15*, 107–142.
44. Juan, W. T., Huang, Z., Hsu, J., Lai, Y., & I, L. (1998). Observation of dust Coulomb clusters in a plasma trap. *Physical Review E*, *58*(6), R6947–R6950.
45. Thomas, H. M., & Morfill, G. E. (1996). Melting dynamics of a plasma crystal. *Nature*, *379*(6568), 806–809.
46. Morfill, G. E., Thomas, H. M., Konopka, U., & Zuzic, M. (1999). The plasma condensation: Liquid and crystalline plasmas. *Physics of Plasmas*, *6*(5), 1769–1780.
47. Konopka, U., Samsonov, D., Ivlev, A. V., Goree, J., Steinberg, V., & Morfill, G. E. (2000). Rigid and differential plasma crystal rotation induced by magnetic fields. *Physical Review E*, *61*(2), 1890–1898.
48. Klindworth, M., Melzer, A., Piel, A., & Schweigert, V. A. (2000). Laser-excited intershell rotation of finite Coulomb clusters in a dusty plasma. *Physical Review B*, *61*(12), 8404–8410.

49. Hou, L. J., Wang, Y. N., & Mišković, Z. L. (2005). Formation and rotation of two-dimensional Coulomb crystals in a magnetized complex plasma. *Physics of Plasmas*, *12*(4), 042104.

50. Paeva, G. V., Dahiya, R. P., Kroesen, G. M. W., & Stoffels, W. W. (2004). Rotation of particles trapped in the sheath of a radio-frequency capacitively coupled plasma. *IEEE Transactions on Plasma Science*, *32*(2), 601–606.

51. Karasev, V. (2006) Rotational motion of dusty structures in glow discharge in longitudinal magnetic field. Yu, Dzlieva, E. S., Ivanov, A. Yu., and Eikhvald, A. I. *Physical Review E*, *74*(6), 066403.

52. Dzlieva, E. S., Karasev, V. Yu., & Eikhval'd, A. I. (2005). The effect of a longitudinal magnetic field on the plasma dust structures in strata in a glow discharge. *Optics and Spectroscopy*, *98*(4), 569–573.

53. Dzlieva, E. S., Karasev, V. Yu., & Éĭkhval'd, A. I. (2006). The onset of rotational motion of dusty plasma structures in strata of a glow discharge in a magnetic field. *Optics and Spectroscopy*, *100*(3), 456–462.

54. Cheung, F., Samarian, A., & James, B. (2003). The rotation of planar-2 to planar-12 dust clusters in an axial magnetic field. *New Journal of Physics*, *5*(1), 75.

55. Vasil'ev, M. M., D'yachkov, L. G., Antipov, S. N., Petrov, O. F., & Fortov, V. E. (2007). Dusty plasma structures in magnetic fields in a d.c. discharge. *JETP Letters*, *86*(6), 358–363.

56. Buss, R. J., & Hareland, W. A. (1994). Gas phase particulate formation in radiofrequency fluorocarbon plasmas. *Plasma Sources Science and Technology*, *3*(3), 268–272.

57. Ganguly, B., Garscadden, A., Williams, J., & Haaland, P. (1993). Growth and morphology of carbon grains. *Journal of Vacuum Science and Technology A*, *11*(4), 1119–1125.

58. Jellum, G. M., Daugherty, J. E., & Graves, D. B. (1991). Particle thermophoresis in low pressure glow discharges. *Journal of Applied Physics*, *69*(10), 6923–6934.

59. Samsonov, D., & Goree, J. (1999). Particle growth in a sputtering discharge. *Journal of Vacuum Science and Technology A*, *17*(5), 2835–2840.
60. Selwyn, G. S., McKillop, J. S., Haller, K. L., & Wu, J. J. (1990). In situ plasma contamination measurements by He–Ne laser light scattering: A case study. *Journal of Vacuum Science and Technology A*, *8*(3), 1726–1731.
61. Choudhary, M., Bergert, R., Mitic, S., & Thoma, M. H. (2020). Three-dimensional dusty plasma in a strong magnetic field: Observation of rotating dust tori. *Physics of Plasmas*, *27*(6), 063701.
62. Schwabe, M., Konopka, U., Bandyopadhyay, P., & Morfill, G. E. (2011). Pattern formation in a complex plasma in high magnetic fields. *Physical Review Letters*, *106*(21), 215004.
63. Carstensen, J., Greiner, F., Block, D., Schablinski, J., Miloch, W. J., & Piel, A. (2012). Charging and coupling of a vertically aligned particle pair in the plasma sheath. *Physics of Plasmas*, *19*(3), 033702.
64. Tadsen, B., Greiner, F., & Piel, A. (2014). Preparation of magnetized nanodusty plasmas in a radio frequency-driven parallel-plate reactor. *Physics of Plasmas*, *21*(10), 103704.
65. Thomas, E., Konopka, U., Artis, D., Lynch, B., Leblanc, S., Adams, S., Merlino, R. L., & Rosenberg, M. (2015). The magnetized dusty plasma experiment (MDPX). *Journal of Plasma Physics*, *81*(2), 345810206.
66. Bates, E. M., Birmingham, W. J., & Romero-Talamas, C. A. (2016). Development of a bitter-type magnet system. *IEEE Transactions on Plasma Science*, *44*(4), 540–544.
67. Dzlieva, E. S., Novikov, L. A., Pavlov, S. I., & Karasev, V. Y. (2018). Direct-current glow discharge dusty plasma in magnetic fields up to 3000 G. *Technical Physics Letters*, *44*(10), 884–886.
68. Melzer, A., Krüger, H., Schütt, S., & Mulsow, M. (2019). Finite dust clusters under strong magnetic fields. *Physics of Plasmas*, *26*(9), 093702.

69. Kompaneets, R., Konopka, U., Ivlev, A. V., Tsytovich, V., & Morfill, G. (2007). Potential around a charged dust particle in a collisional sheath. *Physics of Plasmas*, *14*(5), Art. no. 052108.
70. Castaldo, C., de Angelis, U., & Tsytovich, V. N. (2006). Screening and attraction of dust particles in plasmas. *Physical Review Letters*, *96*(7), Art. no. 075004.
71. Ratynskaia, S., de Angelis, U., Khrapak, S., Klumov, B., & Morfill, G. E. (2006). Electrostatic interaction between dust particles in weakly ionized complex plasmas. *Physics of Plasmas*, *13*(10), 104508.
72. Lampe, M., Joyce, G., Ganguli, G., & Gavrishchaka, V. (2000). Interactions between dust grains in a dusty plasma. *Physics of Plasmas*, *7*(10), 3851.
73. Semenov, I. L., Khrapak, S. A., & Thomas, H. M. (2015). Approximate expression for the electric potential around an absorbing particle in isotropic collisionless plasma. *Physics of Plasmas*, *22*(5), 053704.
74. Filippov, A. V. (2009). Electrostatic interaction of spherical microparticles in dusty plasmas. *Contributions to Plasma Physics*, *49*(7–8), 431–445.
75. Bystrenko, T., & Zagorodny, A. (2002). Effects of bound states in the screening of dust particles in plasmas. *Physics Letters A*, *299*(4), 383–391.
76. Kilgore, M. D., Daugherty, J. E., Porteous, R. K., & Graves, D. B. (1993). Ion drag on an isolated particulate in a low-pressure discharge. *Journal of Applied Physics*, *73*(11), 7195–7202.
77. Bittencourt, J. A. (2004). *Fundamentals of plasma physics*. Springer.
78. Khrapak, S. A., Ivlev, A. V., Morfill, G. E., & Zhdanov, S. K. (2003). Scattering in the attractive Yukawa potential in the limit of strong interaction. *Physical Review Letters*, *90*(22), Art. no. 225002.
79. Khrapak, S. A., Ivlev, A. V., & Morfill, G. E. (2004). Momentum transfer in complex plasmas. *Physical Review E*, *70*(5), Art. no. 056405.
80. Semenov, I. L., Khrapak, S. A., & Thomas, H. M. (2017). Momentum transfer cross-section for ion scattering on dust particles. *Physics of Plasmas*, *24*(3), Art. no. 033710.

81. Khrapak, S. A., Ivlev, A. V., Morfill, G. E., Zhdanov, S. K., & Thomas, H. M. (2004). Scattering in the attractive Yukawa potential: Application to the ion-drag force in complex plasmas. *IEEE Transactions on Plasma Science*, *32*(2), 555–560.

CHAPTER 5

DUST ACOUSTIC INSTABILITY: A QUANTITATIVE ANALYSIS IN PRESENCE OF MAGNETIC FIELD

5.1. INTRODUCTION

Waves and oscillations are one of the powerful information tools about any dynamical system. Dusty plasma is one such kind of dynamical systems where oscillations of charged particles (electrons and ions) develops the propagation of waves at a low frequency range. Further, charged dust particles too participate in the development of waves due to large dust inertia compared to other charged species in the dusty plasma system. When Ikezi predicted the Coulomb crystallization of dust particles in plasma, the immediate response physicist Rao *et al.* was to observe the charged dust particle oscillations and theoretical understanding of dust acoustic wave (DAW) phenomena. After a while, the laboratory setup of dusty plasma and experiments initiated to develop for only observation of dust particles phenomena in plasma. For three decades, there has been extensive research on DAW for various dusty plasma systems, see review paper Ref [1] both theoretical and experimental. DAW in presence of magnetic field in dusty plasma is also observed; see Ref [2].

In the environment of charged plasma species (electrons & ions) and charged dust particles, the dusty plasma system becomes strongly coupled, such that the electrostatic interaction between neighboring dust particles is larger than the thermal/kinetic energy of the charged dust particles [1]. This can be defined by a parameter called Coulomb coupling parameter (Γ) which is the ratio of electrostatic energy between dust to the kinetic energy of dust given as $\Gamma = Z_d^2 e^2/aT_d$. Z_d is the number of charges accumulated or collected by the dust particles, which is generally given by OML theory. Here 'a' is the Wigner-Seitz radius for a three-dimensional system is given as $a^3 = 3/4\,\pi n_d$, where n_d is the number of dust density and T_d is the dust temperature. For the effective screened potential or Yukawa potential, coupling parameter can be written as $\Gamma_d = \Gamma e^{-\kappa}$, where κ is the screening parameter given as a/λ_d. For $\Gamma_d \ll 1$, the dusty plasma system is in strongly coupled liquid phase but less than the requirement of crystallization (~170) [3].

Number of plasma systems shows the existence of dusty plasma in strongly coupled liquid state [4-6]. Most of the studies or experiments have been carried out in crystalline state [7, 8] and in recent times, the liquid phase has been getting more attention [9-11]. In colloidal systems, large friction is due to liquids exerting on the charged particles whereas in dusty plasmas friction is due to the gaseous background on charge particle dynamics and simultaneously on wave dynamics. Effects of the strong coupling on dust acoustic wave (DAW) dispersion relation has been observed in number of theoretical studies [5, 12], such as decreasing of phase speed and frequency, compared to the weakly coupled dusty plasma [13-16]. Instabilities of DAW too affected by strong coupling dusty plasma system [17-19]. Monte Carlo simulations [20-23] and Molecular dynamics [24-26] are the effective simulation tool to understand the dynamics of charged dust particles such as crystallization, phase structures, collective modes, correlation functions etc., in dusty plasma. There are two ways to analyze the DAW instability or excitation, i.e., fluid theory [27-29] and kinetic theory [30-32]. Further, it is established that dust acoustic instability (DAI) is due to the streaming of ions with drift velocity greater than the phase speed of the wave. Besides, phase velocity is less than the ion thermal speed i.e., flow of subthermal ions [30, 33-35].

The present work has been inspired from Rosenberg et al. (2014) where authors have analyzed the growth rate of DAI through strong coupling of dust particles [36]. They have used a different method termed as quasi-localized charge approximation (QLCA), which was generally first used by Rosenberg and Kalman (1997) [13]. Basics of QLCA is to describe the strongly correlated particles or strongly interacting system strapped in a fluctuating potential for a time. A brief review of QLCA for various plasma systems is given in Golden and Kalman (2000) [15]. In this work, QLCA method will be used to study the growth rate of DAI in magnetized strongly coupled dusty plasma with various magnetic fields and coupling parameter. Lastly, an overview of the studies of DAI with various method and need of quantitative analysis of DAW is presented.

5.2. ANALYSIS

Dust particles of negatively charged interacting via Yukawa potential is assumed and the background plasma provides screening. The equilibrium charge neutrality condition is given as

$$n_i = n_e + Z_d n_d \tag{5.1}$$

where n_j is the density of plasma species and dust ($j = e, i, d$). Electrons and ions are considered as Boltzmann distribution. The dispersion relation of longitudinal modes for strongly coupled dusty plasma is given as [13, 14, 38]

$$\epsilon_L(k,\omega) = 1 + \sum_j \chi_j - \frac{\Omega_{L0}^2}{\omega(\omega + i\nu_{th,d}) - D_L(k)} \approx 0 \tag{5.2}$$

where χ_j is the susceptibility of the charged species in plasma. The second term represents the strong coupling of dust particles. Ω_{L0} is the longitudinal DAW frequency in weakly coupled phase given as $\Omega_{L0} = k\lambda_D \omega_{pd}/(1 + k^2\lambda_D^2)^{1/2}$, where ω_{pd} is the dust plasma frequency $= (4\pi Z_d^2 n_d/m_d)^{1/2}$, m_d is the mass of the dust. $D_L(k)$ is the dynamical matrix for the longitudinal modes given as [14, 16]

$$D_L(k) = \frac{n_d}{m_d} \int d^3 r \phi(r) \left(e^{ik.r} - 1\right) g(r) \tag{5.3}$$

where $\phi(r) = (Z_d^2 e^2/r) e^{-r/\lambda_D}$ is the Yukawa potential and $g(r)$ is the equilibrium correlation function. A detailed explicit expression is given in Ref [14, 16]. Kalman and Golden (1990) first proposed the QLCA method for the analysis of dispersion relation in strongly coupled plasma and full detailed explicit expression can be obtained from the paper [37]. Susceptibilities of charged species is given as

$$\chi_e = \frac{1}{k^2 \lambda_{De}^2} \left[1 + \frac{\omega}{\sqrt{2} k_z v_{th,e}} \sum_{-\infty}^{\infty} Z(\zeta_e) \Gamma_{pe} \right] \tag{5.4}$$

$$\chi_i = \frac{1}{k^2 \lambda_{Di}^2} \left[1 + \frac{\omega}{\sqrt{2} k_z v_{th,i}} \sum_{-\infty}^{\infty} Z(\zeta_i) \Gamma_{pi} \right] \tag{5.5}$$

$$\chi_d = \frac{1}{k^2 \lambda_{Dd}^2} \left[1 + \frac{\omega}{\sqrt{2} k_z v_{th,d}} \sum_{-\infty}^{\infty} Z(\zeta_d) \Gamma_{pd} \right] \tag{5.6}$$

$Z(\zeta_j)$ is the plasma dispersion function [39] is a complex valued function Z having complex variable ($\zeta = x + iy$) which describes the propagation of waves in plasma having Maxwellian velocity distribution. In the presence of magnetic field, drift velocity is parallel to the magnetic field, proposed ζ_j is given as

$$\zeta_e = \frac{\omega + k V_{0e} - p\rho_e + i v_e}{\sqrt{2} k_z v_{th,e}} \tag{5.7}$$

$$\zeta_i = \frac{\omega - k V_{0i} + p\rho_i + i v_i}{\sqrt{2} k_z v_{th,i}} \tag{5.8}$$

$$\zeta_d = \frac{\omega - p\rho_d + i v_d}{\sqrt{2} k_z v_{th,d}} \tag{5.9}$$

V_{0j} is the streaming velocity of charged plasma species (e, i, d) and υ_j is the collision frequency of the plasma species. $v_{th,j}$ is the thermal velocity $\sqrt{T_j/m_j}$, where T_j is the temperature and mass (m_j). k_z ($k_\perp$) is the wave vector component along (perpendicular) the external magnetic field $\boldsymbol{B} = B\hat{\boldsymbol{z}}$. $\Gamma_{pj} = I_p(\alpha_j)e^{-\alpha_j}$, where I_p is the modified Bessel function of order p and $\alpha_j = k_\perp^2 v_{th,j}^2/\rho_j^2$, ρ_j is the gyrofrequencies of plasma species qB/m_j. Therefore, the dispersion function for Im $\zeta > 0$,

$$Z(\zeta) = 2i\, exp(-\zeta^2) \int_{-\infty}^{i\zeta} exp(-t^2)\, dt \qquad (5.10)$$

The variable ζ is said to be the ratio of phase velocity of wave to the thermal velocity. Above expressions can be simplified for small and large ζ as,

$$for\ small\ \zeta \quad Z(\zeta) \approx i\sqrt{\pi}exp(-\zeta^2) - 2\zeta\left[1 - \frac{2\zeta^2}{3} + \frac{4\zeta^4}{15} - \frac{8\zeta^6}{105} + \cdots\right] \quad (5.11)$$

$$for\ large\ \zeta \quad Z(\zeta) \approx i\sqrt{\pi}\sigma exp(-\zeta^2) - \frac{1}{\zeta}\left[1 + \frac{1}{2\zeta^2} + \frac{3}{4\zeta^4} + \frac{15}{8\zeta^6} + \cdots\right] \quad (5.12)$$

$$where\ \sigma = \begin{cases} 0 & y > \frac{1}{|x|} \\ 1 & |y| < \frac{1}{|x|} \\ 2 & y < -\frac{1}{|x|} \end{cases} \quad for\ x > 0$$

Condition for kinetic limit is $\zeta_j \ll 1$, implying that wavelength of DAW is very much less than collisional mean free path of electrons and ions. DAI is driven by ion instability i.e., $V_{0i}/v_{th,i} \gg V_{0e}/v_{th,e}$. Dust thermal effects has been neglected for $\Gamma \gg 1$. The analytical solutions of above equations need to be solved and observe the growth rate of DA waves in magnetized strongly coupled dusty plasma.

5.3. SUMMARY & REVIEWS OF WORK.

In Jiang *et al.* (2007), the proposed dispersion relation doesn't satisfy for long wavelength i.e., small k which is the essential to find the acoustic waves [40]. Further, authors have not employed the kinetic theory of QLCA. Golden *et al.* (1993) has calculated the dielectric tensor of the collective modes of the plasma by the method of QLCA where magnetic field is applied perpendicular to the 2D layer of dust particles [41]. Dispersion relation obtained is almost similar to Rosenberg *et al.* (2014) for larger wavelength ($k << 1$). Bonitz *et al.* (2010) theoretically modeled the dispersion function for 2D systems in the presence of magnetic field perpendicular to the plane and strong correlations of dusty plasma [42]. Hou *et al.* (2009) tried to explain the different methodologies for wave spectra of 2D Yukawa systems such as random phase approximation, QLCA and harmonic approximation in presence of external perpendicular magnetic field [43]. Kahler *et al.* (2013) explicitly explained and presented the wave spectrum equations of QLCA in magnetized dusty plasma system [44]. The importance of high frequency modes in strongly coupled magnetized one component plasma (OCP) is shown by Ott *et al.* (2011) [45]. Not much development or investigation hasn't initiated in the studies of kinetic theory of strongly coupled magnetized dusty plasma. Although the above-mentioned major development can be continued and comparisons studies of fluid and kinetic theory can be formulated. Further, most of the work has been the use of redundant equations which need to be addressed for the development of plasma wave theory.

Susceptibility Eqn. (5.4) – (5.6) is the modified equation of Ossakow *et al.* (1975) [46] and Bharuthram & Pather (1997) [38], which includes the strong coupling of dust particle in magnetized plasma. Kinetic theory of DAI requires a lot of complex and rigorous analytical approach. Variables such as dynamical matrix ($D_L(k)$) needs to analyze explicitly for longer wavelengths for dust acoustic modes. Modified Bessel function of order $p=1$ where dust particles get magnetized at very high magnetic field is required to solve the equations. For most of the kinetic

QLCA theory establishment, Maxwellian velocity distribution is considered whereas for DAI can be investigated for Kappa velocity distribution. Since most of the plasma is in natural space environment such as astrophysical plasmas, planetary magnetospheres, solar wind, in which non-Maxwellian high energetic particle is observed. More studies is required to validate this concept both numerically and experimentally and that would be considered as future course of studies.

REFERENCES

1. Merlino, R. L. (2014). 25 years of dust acoustic waves. *Journal of Plasma Physics*, *80*(6), 773–786.
2. Melzer, A., Krüger, H., Maier, D., & Schütt, S. (2021). Physics of magnetized dusty plasmas. *Reviews of Modern Plasma Physics*, *5*(1), 1–29.
3. Hamaguchi, S., Farouki, R. T., & Dubin, D. H. E. (1996). Phase diagram of Yukawa systems near the one-component-plasma limit revisited. *Journal of Chemical Physics*, *105*(17), 7641–7647.
4. Shukla, P. K., & Eliasson, B. (2009). Colloquium: Fundamentals of dust-plasma interactions. *Reviews of Modern Physics*, *81*(1), 25–44.
5. Fortov, V. E., Ivlev, A. V., Khrapak, S. A., Khrapak, A. G., & Morfill, G. E. (2005). Complex (dusty) plasmas: Current status, open issues, perspectives. *Physics Reports*, *421*(1–2), 1–103.
6. Ishihara, O. (2007). Complex plasma: Dusts in plasma. *Journal of Physics D: Applied Physics*, *40*(8), R121–R147.
7. Thomas, H., Morfill, G. E., Demmel, V., Goree, J., Feuerbacher, B., & Möhlmann, D. (1994). Plasma crystal: Coulomb crystallization in a dusty plasma. *Physical Review Letters*, *73*(5), 652–655.
8. Thoma, M. H., Kretschmer, M., Rothermel, H., Thomas, H. M., & Morfill, G. E. (2005). The plasma crystal. *American Journal of Physics*, *73*(5), 420–424.

9. Nosenko, V., & Goree, J. (2004). Shear flows and shear viscosity in a two-dimensional Yukawa system (dusty plasma). *Physical Review Letters*, *93*(15), 155004.
10. Nunomura, S., Zhdanov, S., Samsonov, D., & Morfill, G. (2005). Wave spectra in solid and liquid complex (dusty) plasmas. *Physical Review Letters*, *94*(4), 045001.
11. Chan, C.-L., Lai, Y.-J., Woon, W.-Y., Chu, H.-Y., & I, L. (2005). Dusty plasma liquids. *Plasma Physics and Controlled Fusion*, *47*(5A), A273–A281.
12. Fortov, V. E., & Morfill, G. E. (2009). *Complex and dusty plasmas: From laboratory to space*. CRC Press.
13. Rosenberg, M., & Kalman, G. (1997). Dust acoustic waves in strongly coupled dusty plasmas. *Physical Review E*, *56*(6), 7166–7173.
14. Kalman, G., Rosenberg, M., & DeWitt, H. E. (2000). Collective modes in strongly correlated Yukawa liquids: Waves in dusty plasmas. *Physical Review Letters*, *84*(26), 6030–6033.
15. Golden, K. I., & Kalman, G. J. (2000). Quasilocalized charge approximation in strongly coupled plasma physics. *Physics of Plasmas*, *7*(1), 14–32.
16. Donkó, Z., Kalman, G. J., & Hartmann, P. (2008). Dynamical correlations and collective excitations of Yukawa liquids. *Journal of Physics: Condensed Matter*, *20*(41), 413101.
17. Rosenberg, M., Kalman, G. J., & Hartmann, P. (2012). Instabilities in Yukawa liquids. *Contributions to Plasma Physics*, *52*(1), 70–73.
18. Kalman, G. J., & Rosenberg, M. (2003). Instabilities in strongly coupled plasmas. *Journal of Physics A: Mathematical and General*, *36*(22), 5963–5969.
19. Rosenberg, M., & Shukla, P. K. (2011). Instabilities in strongly coupled ultracold neutral plasmas. *Physica Scripta*, *83*(1), 015503.

20. Stringfellow, G. S., DeWitt, H. E., & Slattery, W. L. (1990). Equation of state of the one-component plasma derived from precision Monte Carlo calculations. *Physical Review A*, *41*(2), 1105–1111.
21. Ichimaru, S., & Shuji, O. (1990). Monte Carlo simulation study of dense plasmas: Freezing, transport and nuclear reaction. In *Strongly coupled plasma physics* (pp. 101–112). Elsevier.
22. Ogata, S., & Ichimaru, S. (1992). Monte Carlo Simulation Study of Dense Plasmas. *Physics of Nonideal Plasmas*, 20-27.
23. Jones, M. D., & Ceperley, D. M. (1996). Crystallization of the one-component plasma at finite temperature. *Physical Review Letters*, *76*(24), 4572–4575.
24. Schmidt, P., Zwicknagel, G., Reinhard, P.-G., & Toepffer, C. (1997). Longitudinal and transversal collective modes in strongly correlated plasmas. *Physical Review E*, *56*(6), 7310–7313.
25. Ohta, H., & Hamaguchi, S. (2000). Wave dispersion relations in Yukawa fluids. *Physical Review Letters*, *84*(26 Pt 1), 6026–6029.
26. Zwicknagel, G. (1999). Molecular dynamics simulations of the dynamics of correlations and relaxation in an OCP. *Contributions to Plasma Physics*, *39*(1–2), 155–158.
27. D'Angelo, N., & Merlino, R. L. (1996). Current-driven dust-acoustic instability in a collisional plasma. *Planetary and Space Science*, *44*(12), 1593–1598.
28. Thomas, Jr., E. (2010). Driven dust acoustic waves with thermal effects: Comparison of experiment to fluid theory. *Physics of Plasmas*, *17*(4), 043701.
29. Suranga Ruhunusiri, W. D., & Goree, J. (2014). Dispersion relations for the dust-acoustic wave under experimental conditions. *Physics of Plasmas*, *21*(5), 053702.
30. Rosenberg, M. (1993). Ion- and dust-acoustic instabilities in dusty plasmas. *Planetary and Space Science*, *41*(3), 229–233.

31. Rosenberg, M. (1996). Ion-dust streaming instability in processing plasmas. *Journal of Vacuum Science and Technology A, 14*(2), 631–633.
32. Melandsø, F., Aslaksen, T. K., & Havnes, O. (1993). A kinetic model for dust acoustic waves applied to planetary rings. *Journal of Geophysical Research: Space Physics, 98*(A8), 13315–13323.
33. Arp, O., Goree, J., & Piel, A. (2012). Particle chains in a dilute dusty plasma with subsonic ion flow. *Physical Review E, 85*(4), 046409.
34. Khrapak, S. A., Ratynskaia, S. V., Zobnin, A. V., Usachev, A. D., Yaroshenko, V. V., Thoma, M. H., Kretschmer, M., Höfner, H., Morfill, G. E., Petrov, O. F., & Fortov, V. E. (2005). Particle charge in the bulk of gas discharges. *Physical Review E, 72*(2), 016406.
35. Fortov, V., Morfill, G., Petrov, O., Thoma, M., Usachev, A., Hoefner, H., Zobnin, A., Kretschmer, M., Ratynskaia, S., Fink, M., Tarantik, K., Gerasimov, Y., & Esenkov, V. (2005). The project "Plasmakristall-4" (PK-4)—A new stage in investigations of dusty plasmas under microgravity conditions: First results and future plans. *Plasma Physics and Controlled Fusion, 47*(12B), B537–B549.
36. Rosenberg, M., Kalman, G. J., Hartmann, P., & Goree, J. (2014). Effect of strong coupling on the dust acoustic instability. *Physical Review E, 89*(1), 013103.
37. Kalman, G., & Golden, K. I. (1990). Response function and plasmon dispersion for strongly coupled Coulomb liquids. *Physical Review A, 41*(10), 5516–5527.
38. Bharunthram, R., & Pather, T. (1996). The kinetic dust-acoustic instability in a magnetized dusty plasma. *Planetary and Space Science, 44*(2), 137–146.
39. Fried, B. D., & Conte, S. D. (2015). *The plasma dispersion function: The Hilbert transform of the Gaussian*. Academic Press.

40. Jiang, K., Song, Y.H., & Wang, Y.-N. (2007). Theoretical study of the wave dispersion relation for a two-dimensional strongly coupled Yukawa system in a magnetic field. *Physics of Plasmas*, *14*(10), 103708.
41. Golden, K. I., Kalman, G., & Wyns, P. (1993). Dielectric tensor and collective modes in a two-dimensional electron liquid in a magnetic field. *Physical Review B*, 48(12), 8882–8889.
42. Bonitz, M., Donkó, Z., Ott, T., Kählert, H., & Hartmann, P. (2010). Nonlinear magnetoplasmons in strongly coupled Yukawa plasmas. *Physical Review Letters*, 105(5), 055002.
43. Hou, L.-J., Shukla, P. K., Piel, A., & Mišković, Z. L. (2009). Wave spectra of two-dimensional Yukawa solids and liquids in the presence of a magnetic field. *Physics of Plasmas*, 16(7), 073704.
44. Kählert, H., Ott, T., Reynolds, A., Kalman, G. J., & Bonitz, M. (2013). Obliquely propagating waves in the magnetized strongly coupled one-component plasma. *Physics of Plasmas*, 20(5), 057301.
45. Ott, T., Kählert, H., Reynolds, A., & Bonitz, M. (2012). Oscillation spectrum of a magnetized strongly coupled one-component plasma. *Physical Review Letters*, 108(25), 255002.
46. Ossakow, S. L., Papadopoulos, K., Orens, J., & Coffey, T. (1975). Parallel propagation effects on the type 1 electrojet instability. *Journal of Geophysical Research*, 80(1), 141–148.

CHAPTER 6

SUMMARY AND FUTURE SCOPE OF WORKS

One of the primary goals of this thesis is to understand the nonlinear behavior of dust particles in plasma in presence and absence of magnetic field. Theoretical understanding of the dust particles characteristics in plasma, especially in magnetized plasma has been limited by complex equations, which requires rigorous and detailed analysis. For this reason, dusty plasmas are also called as Complex plasmas. A significant amount of study is being done experimentally in magnetized plasma with dust particles, to observe various phenomena such as low frequency waves, dust particle phase transition of solid/liquid, electron depletion instability, dust crystals/voids, etc. However, a limited amount of theoretical work has been proposed. In this thesis, some of the problems associated with dust particles has been explored theoretically and verified with experimental observations with certain limitations. Nature of these works gives insight into the theoretical aspect of the basic behavior of dust particles in plasma or magnetized plasma, which lays the foundation work for better analyzing equations and provide a generalized theory.

Outcome of Objective 1

Plasma potential, floating potential, electron temperature, and plasma density are the parameters measured from characterization of plasma. This provides the sufficient information about the plasma in a particular confined space of experimental setup. The measurement can be made in axial and radial direction of device. The probe is inserted into the plasma chamber and current is collected from plasma with varying voltage. From I-V curve, plasma parameters can be measured through OML theory. Three different probe technique have been used Langmuir probe, Emissive probe, and double Langmuir probe, which are designed, fabricated and installed on the DPEx-II device. For all three cases, measurement was taken at three discharge voltage and pressure. Langmuir probe is a simple metallic metal of 10 mm length and 1 mm diameter, screened axially along the chamber above the cathode. For a 40 cm length of cathode, I-V curve is plotted for each point varied 1 cm apart. Langmuir probe gives the measure of all plasma parameters with the help of MATLAB programming.

Discharge voltage is varied from 275 V to 375 V, while working pressure is varied from 0.1 mbar to 0.14 mbar. Keeping pressure as a constant at 0.12 mbar and varying discharge voltage, the change in plasma parameters can be observed. T_e decreases as voltage increases due to frequent collisions of electrons with plasma species. Instead of acquiring energy from the electric field, the energy is transferred to plasma species. From the OML theory, it is observed that T_e is inversely proportional to n_e, hence n_e increases with discharge voltage. As frequent collisions increase the rate of ionization in plasma. Floating potential and plasma potential increases with increase in discharge voltage. This can be attributed to the presence of energetic electrons reaching the probe. Most of the plasma parameters can be approximated by the Langmuir probe. However, for accurate measurement of plasma and floating potential, Emissive probe is used where electrons are emitted from the probe and plasma currents are collected in relation with the rate of emission. It is a thin wire (0.125 mm diameter) coiled at the edge of ceramic tube in a semicircle form and current is passed through the wire for emission of electrons. Generally, there are three ways of measuring the plasma potential from emissive probe, i.e., floating point method, separation point method and inflation point method. Separation point method and inflation method might overestimate or underestimate from actual potential measurements due to the methods they are used. Floating-point method gives a straightforward measurement where the measurements of potential are saturated with further emission of electrons from the probe. However, many researchers have argued the formation of virtual cathode at higher emission might hinder the accurate measurement of potential. Further, it was realized that the margin of error (T_e/e) might be very less compared to how accurately the potential is determined. With the formula from OML theory, through measured plasma potential other parameters too can be determined. There is a more robust and elegant way of measuring the electron temperature rather than finding from the formula, i.e., double Langmuir probe. It is a probe of two-tungsten wire of same diameter and separated by a distance greater than the Debye length of the plasma. Because, while measuring the currents from plasma Debye sphere formed around probe should not overlap with the adjacent probe. Double Langmuir probe gives the direct measurement of electron temperature from the symmetry I-V curve. Due to the asymmetrical design of electrodes in DPEx-II, the presence of ionization instability did made difference in Langmuir measurements. That is the reason; there is large fluctuations or error bar in the graph. Reason for having asymmetrical design of electrodes is to slow down the ion streaming to the cathode such that melting of dust particles can be avoided. Further, to observe the stable dust crystallization in DC glow discharge plasma at a stable potential above the cathode.

Outcome of Objective 2

Hindrance of measuring plasma potential in plasma through emissive probe has been one of the rigorous studies faced by researchers. Virtual cathode formed due to emission of electrons from the probe is one of culprit in this type of measurement. A negative potential is formed near the probe/wall which does act as cathode and hence the name 'Virtual Cathode'. Due to this, a double layer potential is also observed near the probe/wall. Dust particles are ambiguous in the plasma system, either it is introduced into the plasma system or dust particles assimilate due to gaseous systems or surface particles eroded from the energetic plasma species. Dust particles levitate near the sheath region of the electrodes once introduced in the plasma. Such dusty plasma systems do change the natural properties or characteristics of plasma. Now, the question was how the dust particles effects the potential in the sheath or whether virtual cathode is feasible in the dusty plasma system. For evaluating the potential profile near a wall or electrode in a weakly coupled dusty plasma system, a mathematical model is put forth. Equations created from this are also used to forecast the circumstances that will lead to the development of a virtual cathode. From theoretical and numerical studies, presence of virtual cathode is predicted at a threshold wall/probe temperature ($T_{w,th}$) 2494 °K ~ 2685 °K in weakly ionized dusty plasma. Further, the stability of virtual cathode formation with different emission is also reported, where with increase of emission the virtual cathode disappears. Analysis has been done with the dust particle potential, just dust charge and no charge. Double layer potential is also observed in the case of no charge taken on dust particles. With different dust density, the formation of virtual cathode is observed at various emission. As emission increases, the threshold wall/probe temperature for formation of virtual cathode increases as shown in the Fig. 3.7. In contrast with the increase in dust density, $T_{w,th}$ shows not much difference. In comparison with the plasma without dust particles, the virtual cathode was observed at $T_{w,th}$ = 1750 °K (Tierno et al (2016)). Therefore, interesting to note that in the presence of dust particles, which collects electrons and ions from the plasma surroundings delays the formation of virtual cathode near the wall/probe. As a result, the increase of $T_{w,th}$ in dusty plasma. In addition, dust particles create double layer formation near the wall/probe. However, not much significant work has been carried out in the magnetized plasma or magnetized dusty plasma, which gives the future prospective to understand the behavior of virtual cathode in these conditions near wall/probe. Meanwhile these works will benefit in understanding the boundary-wall interaction in a finite length plasma.

Outcome of Objective 3

Dust particles acquires charges from the plasma and float or levitate at certain potential depending on the discharge parameters. In dusty plasma, dust particles levitate and forms a crystal-like structure, which is also observed experimentally. However, these dust particles can be harmful in fusion reactors, magnetron sputtering, or semiconductor chip processing. On the perspective of material science, crystallization growth of dust particles in plasma offers a broad spectrum to analyze and benefit from it. Hence, evolution of crystallization of dust particles especially in presence of external magnetic field is studied through numerical and simulation. For the simulation of DC discharge plasma with levitated dust particles, a novel mathematical analysis is presented and validated using COMSOL Multiphysics software. It is observed at electric field of 6 V, the dust particles levitate above the electrodes keeping magnetic field (applied along the electric field) zero. As magnetic field (B) is increased the dust particles becomes closer to neighboring particles since the plasma species currents becomes more streamlined along the field lines of B. Further, charging currents to the dust particles is reduced due to decrease in Larmor radius of plasma species. At $B = 1T$, the dust particles come close to each other forming a crystal-like structure with multilayers. At $B > 1T$, dust particles start moving towards the center of chamber and upwards to the anode. All these phenomena are quantized in terms of scattering cross-section of the dust particles with neighboring dust particles. Hence, as B increases the scattering cross-section of dust particles decreases. A mathematical equation is also introduced where the scattering cross-section of dust particles is found and validated with the given simulation results. Parameters, such as surface potential of dust particles is given in presence of B, which plays a major role in defining the behavior of dust particles. It is shown that both theoretical and simulation results have same results. Further, the graph and equations show surface potential exponentially decreasing with B. Experimentally in many plasmas, it is observed that as B increases the dust particles forms the crystal-like structure. In some cases, there is an observation of solid/liquid phase transition, which is separate large topic to discuss. Therefore, the foundation for the theoretical aspect of charge dust particles crystal like structure is established. Further, these equations can be improved with more sophisticated dust potential with screening length, anisotropic charging currents to the dust and scattering cross-section of many body systems.

Outcome of Objective 4

Apart from the forming crystal like structure, charged dust particles also introduces low frequency acoustic waves only due to massive dust particles compared to the other plasma species components. For decades, researchers have investigated the rigorous studies of dust acoustic waves (DAW) for various dusty plasma and magnetized dusty plasma systems. Nonlinear studies such as solitary waves and shock structures is determined through the famous KdV-Burger's equation. Experimentally these nonlinear phenomena have been observed in both laboratory DC and RF plasma. Charged dust particles also shows the behavior of strong coupling (Γ), which determines the crystallization of dust particles in plasma system. For $1 \ll \Gamma \ll 172$ values, the dust particles behave as a solid/liquid phase also called as Yukawa liquids system because the interaction between charged dust particles is mainly described by Yukawa potential. Generally, there are two regimes which are used to study the DA wave phenomena i.e., fluid, and kinetic regime. Larger section of studies has been carried out with fluid or hydrodynamic equations with various plasma systems. Whereas for kinematic regime using Vlasov equations, has also been carried with much vigor. However, many review publications have described beautifully on the works of DAW but there is not much development on quantitative analysis of DAW. Kalman & Golden (1990) developed Quasi-localized Charge Approximation (QLCA) for the study of dielectric response of strongly coupled dusty plasma. QLCA is used to study the DA instability (DAI) in magnetized strongly coupled dusty plasma systems. In this work, a new mathematical model is presented in a strongly coupled magnetized dusty plasma system with a kinetic regime. Major reason for using QLCA is to determine the interaction of charged dust particles with neighboring dust particles in terms of Yukawa potential. Growth rate and damping rate of DAI has been studied through QLCA method and compared with the other methods.

FUTURE SCOPE OF THIS THESIS

The experimental characterization of DPEx-II present in this thesis can form the basis for the study of dust crystallization, Yukawa liquids, low frequency waves, phase transitions of dust particles and these studies can be carry forwarded in the presence of magnetic field (B) in a DC glow discharge plasma. Hindrance in measurement of plasma potential from probe diagnostics due to the formation of virtual cathode is well known concept. However, studies of virtual cathode in dusty plasma system are not explored completely. In this thesis, formation of virtual cathode is studied numerically in a weakly coupled dusty plasma system. This theory can be developed more robust with the presence of B in a dusty plasma system and verify with the experimental studies. Significance of this work will be more helpful in studies of large plasma devices. Additionally, the explicit dependence of dust surface potential on virtual cathode formation is not discussed, which also can be included in the equations and study the influence on virtual cathode. Scattering cross-section equation can be improved by correct approximation of impact radius of dust particles and developing more robust equations. Furthermore, rotation of dust particles has not been considered in the present work, which also can be included in future studies. Quantitative analysis of DAW is very necessary at this time since lot of articles has been published in fluid and kinetic theory with various dusty plasma systems. Assumptions, approximations, and higher order differential equations in solving DAW need to be inspected and to develop a conclusive theory. Whereas experimental studies of low frequency electromagnetic waves and observation is still challenging.

www.ingramcontent.com/pod-product-compliance
Lightning Source LLC
LaVergne TN
LVHW010226070526
838199LV00062B/4728